THE RIGHT TO DIE

OTHER BOOKS BY GARY BAUSLAUGH

Robert Latimer — A Story of Justice and Mercy (2010)
The Secret Power of Juries (2013)
Voices of Humanism (2014)
A Search for Better University Education (2015)
Travels with Shakespeare (2015)

THE RIGHT TO DIE

THE COURAGEOUS CANADIANS WHO GAVE US THE RIGHT TO A DIGNIFIED DEATH

GARY BAUSLAUGH

JAMES LORIMER & COMPANY LTD., PUBLISHERS
TORONTO

James Lorimer & Company Ltd., Publishers acknowledges the support of the Ontario Arts Council. We acknowledge the support of the Canada Council for the Arts which last year invested $24.3 million in writing and publishing throughout Canada. We acknowledge the Government of Ontario through the Ontario Media Development Corporation's Ontario Book Initiative.

  Canadä

Cover design: Meredith Bangay
Cover image: Shutterstock

Library and Archives Canada Cataloguing in Publication

Bauslaugh, Gary, author
    The right to die : the courageous Canadians who gave us the right to a dignified death / Gary Bauslaugh.

Includes bibliographical references and index.
Issued in print and electronic formats.
ISBN 978-1-4594-1116-6 (hardback).--ISBN 978-1-4594-1117-3 (epub)

    1. Right to die--Canada. 2. Assisted suicide--Canada. I. Title.

R726.B339 2016   179.7   C2016-900040-0
                                                     C2016-900041-9

James Lorimer & Company Ltd., Publishers
117 Peter Street, Suite 304
Toronto, ON, Canada
M5V 2G9
www.lorimer.ca

Printed and bound in Canada.

This book is dedicated to:
Emily Bronwyn Bauslaugh
and
Arnold Preston Bauslaugh
both of whom died too young.

To everything there is a season,
a time to live, and a time to die . . .
Ecclesiastes 3

Nothing can make injustice just but mercy.
Robert Frost

CONTENTS

INTRODUCTION
ON MATTERS OF LIFE, DEATH AND THE LAW

"I want to die as well as my cat did a few years ago," Allan Scott of Victoria wrote in a letter to the *Victoria Times Colonist* newspaper in October 2014. Scott was dying of lung cancer and, while at peace with knowing that he had a terminal illness, he was dreading three things, which he felt were almost inevitable:

- unnecessary, prolonged physical and psychological distress,
- unnecessary, large monetary costs to his family and to the health care system and
- unnecessary loss of dignity.

Scott described how he and his family handled the death of his cat:

We did the kindest thing possible — we took him
to a vet, who administered a painless [life-ending]
injection while he was being stroked. I ask no more
for myself. Well, maybe a good Scotch beforehand.

* * *

Versions of Scott's lament have been heard repeatedly, every day, across our country, as people with terminal illnesses face not just death but the more frightening prospect of a gruesome, prolonged and painful death, a death that most of us would not accept for our pets.

In past years we have, through a Canadian law prohibiting assisted death under any circumstances, made Scott's simple wish very difficult to fulfill. In February 2015, however, the Supreme Court of Canada ruled this absolute prohibition of assisted death to be unconstitutional, and as of February 2016 some form of it was to be legalized.

This change in the law is not a trivial one: it changes a long-established prohibition in a way that will affect the lives of thousands of Canadians. Any of us could be affected by this change and many of us will be.

The change came in spite of strong and sustained opposition that had its roots in religious teachings about the sanctity of life, but also in bitter human experience of situations where human life has been held to be of little or no value. We need look no further than the mass killings and genocides that have darkened recent world history.

Those who rail against devaluing life in any way have a point. We cannot ever afford to take lightly the matter of intentional causing of death.

Yet, Allan Scott had a point too: untold numbers of

desperately ill Canadians too sick or too disabled — or simply not knowing how — to end their own lives have suffered needlessly and grievously because of this prohibition on getting assistance. Suicide is legal in Canada, but that has not meant that it has been readily available to many Canadians.

How did we get beyond our fears to the point where the Supreme Court of Canada could unanimously vote to strike down the ban on assisted suicide? It was a long process, extending over many decades, and it did not happen in a vacuum. It took courageous actions of many Canadians, and it took the heartfelt protests of many others. These Canadians, collectively, helped lead public awareness to the point where the decriminalization of assisted suicide became possible.

This book tells some of the stories of those whose actions and words helped us move to a more nuanced view of the respect for life, recognizing that sometimes such respect entails facilitating the easeful departure from a life that has become worse than death.

* * *

Two distinct types of assisted death — giving aid to a suffering person who wants to terminate his or her life — will be referred to throughout this book. *Assisted suicide* is when someone helps a suicide take place by, for example, providing a lethal dose of pills to the dying person, who then takes the pills himself or herself. A particular form of this is called *physician-assisted suicide*, where a doctor is providing the assistance. *Euthanasia*, on the other hand, is a process whereby someone other than the dying person takes the final action to cause death. This might, for example, be a lethal injection administered by a physician at the request of the patient. Assisted death refers to either assisted suicide or this sort of voluntary euthanasia.

In the past the law has made a sharp distinction between assisted suicide and voluntary euthanasia. Assisted suicide has had its own legal statute (Section 241(b) of the *Criminal Code*, discussed later), while euthanasia, even when requested by the dying person, has been treated as murder.

However, a logical distinction between these two kinds of assisted death is difficult to make. A doctor might insert a syringe, holding a lethal dose of a medication, into the arm of a dying patient. If the patient pushed the plunger in and then dies, then that would be physician-assisted suicide. But if the doctor pushed in the plunger, it would be euthanasia.

A doctor might hold a glass filled with a lethal liquid mixture to the lips of a paralyzed patient and pour it into his or her mouth after the patient has somehow indicated the wish to die. The patient can then spit out the liquid or swallow it. If the patient swallows it and dies, is that assisted suicide? Is it euthanasia? Does it matter? Much is often made of the supposed difference between the two — that while assisted suicide is one thing, voluntary euthanasia represents, to some, crossing a moral Rubicon. But to many, including me, these two acts, whoever takes the very final action, are morally equivalent.

Some further clarification of terms might be helpful. *Active euthanasia* is the taking of direct steps to end a life, such as injecting a lethal dose of some drug and pushing the plunger as in the example above. If this is done at the behest of the dying person, then it is called voluntary active euthanasia. That is the form of euthanasia that many see as morally equivalent to assisted suicide. Both involve hastening death at the bidding of the patient.

Passive euthanasia is ending a life, not by taking active steps to bring about death, but by the cessation of treatment that is keeping the patient alive. Sometimes called "pulling the plug," this form of euthanasia, when voluntary (done in accordance with the wish of the patient), is considered legal in Canada. It is difficult, here as well, to find a significant moral distinction between two similar acts — between active and passive euthanasia: both involve the intentional causing of death in circumstances where it is warranted by the wish of the patient and by extreme suffering. However, active euthanasia, even when voluntary, has traditionally been regarded as murder, while passive euthanasia has been deemed acceptable in Canada.

The most controversial type of euthanasia is when the dying person has not given or is not able to give his or her consent or is unwilling to give such consent. The former is referred to as *non-voluntary euthanasia* and the latter as *involuntary euthanasia*. Both of these are much more problematic, ethically, than voluntary euthanasia.

Even without consent, however, there is the odd case where a compelling argument can be made for non-voluntary euthanasia. You will encounter, for example, the heartbreaking story of young Christopher Ramberg in Chapter 1. Such cases, often called "mercy killings," are technically murders, but in fact truly can be acts of human kindness, not malice. However, as much as such cases have elicited sympathy for all those involved, and have affected the general growing acceptance of some forms of assisted death, under the law, mercy killing remains murder.

Canada is trying to become a more merciful country. This book celebrates what has been achieved in Canada, which is official acceptance of the idea of assisted death, and it celebrates those who have helped us get to where we are.

CHAPTER 1

FORTY SHADES OF MERCY

Many people have a story about a friend or relative who suffered through a prolonged and unwanted dying process, or resorted to desperate, sometimes violent, measures to find relief. In his deposition to the 2012 B.C. Supreme Court case on assisted death (see Chapter 6), John Dixon of the B.C. Civil Liberties Association tells the story of the grim death of his friend Norman Hope in 1981.

> *I knew Norman Hope for about 15 years, as we were both members of a small land and housing cooperative in Desolation Sound, British Columbia. Norman was a retired logger and store keeper. He was a lifelong smoker and heavy drinker. In 1980, he developed oesophageal cancer, which eventually metastasized; he died one year*

later, after significant suffering.

When he became ill, both he and his wife, Doris, were adamant that as he neared death, he would remain in his home in Refuge Cove, and die in the care of his wife and friends. He was a very intelligent man, with a wry sense of humour. Once, when I remarked upon his continuing ability, notwithstanding the terrible pain of his throat cancer, to enjoy rye whisky and conversation, he retorted that he "was the Terry Fox of alcoholism." Unhappily, his disease did not share his sense of humour, and gradually but inexorably, terrible pain became insupportable pain, and we had to face the fact that only a hospital could provide the resources that could mitigate his agony. And so he was moved, first to Vancouver General Hospital, and finally to the University of British Columbia Hospital.

Once he was in Vancouver, I visited Norman often, as Vancouver General Hospital stood between my home and the college where I worked as a professor. Even though he was able to receive better pain management in the hospital, Norman's life had become a world of oxygen masks, intravenous tubes, stupefying drugs and incontinence pads. As the cancer ruthlessly advanced, Norman rejected the terms upon which his life was being preserved for him. He made it clear to me that he desired assistance in dying, saying to me, "If you weren't such a [expletive] coward, Dixon, you would bring me something, anything to help me die. That's what I need from you, and you know it."

I was, however, afraid to help him. I had no scruples about the morality of assisting his suicide. Rather, I was afraid of the potential criminal liability associated with helping him die, and the consequences for myself. Norman knew me well, and he was right to accuse me of being more selfish than principled.

Troubled by my inability to carry out Norman's wishes, I asked one of the physicians caring for Norman what he would do in my place. I was astonished by his advice. "If Norman was my father, I would hustle him out of here as quickly as possible, take him to a safe place, and help him die."

Eventually, Norman was moved to the University of British Columbia Hospital, which had facilities for the terminally ill which were not available at Vancouver General Hospital at that time. Within a few days of his transfer, it was apparent that he was nearing death, and I responded to a call from Doris to join her at Norman's side.

When I arrived, the hospital had already withdrawn Norman's life support. He was so dehydrated that there were no tears to lubricate his eyes, and they were locked open in a fixed and startled stare, scaled over with a translucent film. He was gasping for breath, moaning and writhing weakly in evident agony. Doris, usually an enormously self-possessed woman, was crying uncontrollably. But we could not help him die. As

Norman continued to struggle for breath, I pulled Norman up from the bed and cradled him in my arms while Doris wept. We rocked on for another 15 minutes or so until Norman finally died in our arms.

I believe that Norman Hope's death agonies both psychic and physical were unnecessarily imposed upon him by the criminal prohibition of counselling or assisting a suicide. I believe that the young physician at VGH, who advised me to help Norman die, was discharging his professional, medical duty to advise me of the best course of action, and courageously exposed himself to the possibility of both criminal prosecution and the loss of his professional status. He took an enormous risk in judging that I was unlikely to betray him.

* * *

Many Canadians have found themselves in circumstances similar to those faced by John Dixon and Norman Hope. Most of those who might have given the merciful gift of hastening death were, like Dixon, justifiably fearful of doing so. They could end up spending years in prison for a brief act of compassion.

There have been some Canadians, however, who fought against the restrictive laws against assisted death and found ways to mitigate and circumvent those laws. Some risked their own freedom to help suffering people die. Even justice system officials, recognizing the evident injustice of strict application of the law, have often been lenient with those who have committed illegal acts of mercy, when it became clear that mercy alone had been the motivation.

Mercy has several distinguishing features. As memorably described by Shakespeare's Portia, it is not "strained" — not given under any sort of compulsion other than the persuasive force of human compassion. It is as restorative "as the gentle rain from heaven upon the place beneath." It is ennobling — "it blesseth him that giveth and him that takes."

Mercy may seem irrelevant amidst the rough exigencies of modern life, yet we find ourselves strangely and powerfully affected by examples of them. The quality of mercy somehow reaches and touches our innermost sense of what is best in the human experience.

The sickroom of a dying person can be a barren place, bereft of hope, without thought of the future. But it can also be, and often is, a place for gifts of kindness. For some, the greatest of those is the gift of mercy.

This book looks at forty stories about Canadian experiences with mercy and assisted death. Collectively, these stories, along with influential statements made by a number of dying people discussed in later chapters, reveal a long Canadian struggle to find a humane and legal means of bestowing mercy upon the terminally afflicted, as well as a broader recognition of the fundamental personal right to choose the time and place of one's own death. All of the events described here helped shape public opinion and moved us closer to the historic breakthrough at the Supreme Court of Canada in 2015.

CHRISTOPHER RAMBERG, 1941

In the morning of December 7, 1941, the Japanese air force bombed Pearl Harbor, and the world changed forever.

Three days later, on December 10, 1941, Victor and

Dorothy Ramberg went to trial in Alberta for an event that changed their lives forever: the killing of their two-and-a-half-year-old son, Victor Christopher Ramberg.

The impact on the world of the first of these two events was vastly larger than the second. But not to the Rambergs. The tragic circumstances of the death of their child, though publicly overshadowed by the scale of the earthshaking events in the Pacific, could be not have been more heart-breaking and compelling for them. Their mostly forgotten story is a quintessential Canadian example of the courage and compassion that is sometimes required for acts of mercy.

Young Victor Christopher Ramberg's problem with one of his eyes became evident at a young age. At some point in the little boy's second year his parents noticed an odd reflection in his right eye, but wanted to think that it was nothing important. Then, in January 1941, before the boy's second birthday, he seemed to be losing his bearings and would bump into furniture. On January 25 they took him to a doctor in Calgary, about thirty-two miles southwest of the Ramberg's home in the village of Keoma, where the father, Victor, worked at the Keoma Wheat Pool elevator just a short distance from the cottage where the family lived.

The doctor could tell immediately that there was some serious problem with the right eye and sent the Rambergs to a Calgary eye specialist, Dr. A. Fettes, who found evidence of a tumour growing in the affected eye. He believed the tumour, which had already destroyed the right eyeball, to be malignant. Young Victor had lost all sight in the right eye, but still had some vision in his left eye.

Dr. Fettes planned to operate the next day, with the intention of removing the damaged eye. The hope was that the removal would get rid of most of the cancerous tissue and that the boy might then be treatable with radiation. However, the Rambergs were about to receive even more devastating news: when the boy was sedated and Dr. Fettes was able to get a better look at his left eye he found that there was a tumour growing there as well. It was not so large as the growth in the right eye, but in all likelihood it would continue to grow and be as destructive as the other. And both tumours would likely continue to expand into the boy's brain cavity and kill the boy.

It would do little good to remove the damaged right eye without taking the left as well. And even then it was likely that it would be difficult to stop the relentless growth of the cancer. The diagnosis, with the discovery of the second tumour, was virtually a death sentence.

One can only imagine the horror felt by the Rambergs on hearing this news. They deeply loved and doted on their child; he was the centre of their lives. And now, unexpectedly, he was dying. There can be no more devastating news for parents.

Given the likelihood of death whatever they did, the Rambergs opted not to have the operation. To understand this decision one must think of trying to cope with the idea that one's child is desperately ill. Taking one eye out is one thing, but both? Taking out the eye that was still functioning? There was something so terribly final about that action that the Rambergs just could not accept it.

The response of the Rambergs to the news about their child reminds me of that of Tracy Latimer's parents (see Chapter 2) when she was diagnosed as needing another in a series of operations, this time to cut off her femurs and remove her hip joints to try to stop the pain of dislocation caused by her spastic and uncontrolled body movements. In spite of the already seriously compromised condition of their daughter, this new operation seemed, to the Latimers, unacceptable. It was a step too far; it seemed like mutilation of their precious daughter. I think the proposed removal of both eyes of little Victor Christopher felt the same way to the Rambergs.

When Dr. Fettes returned from giving the grim task of giving the bad news to the parents — that both eyes were affected — he said to one of his colleagues: "No, they won't have both eyes out, and we have told them this child probably will have terrific pain while it lives."

The Rambergs took their little boy home and cared for him devotedly as his condition worsened. While he was not in much pain at first, discomfort grew and the pressure of the growing tumours pressed against his eyeballs and his brain. At the beginning of October Dr. Fettes again saw the boy, who by this time had completely lost the vision in both eyes and was experiencing a lot of pain. He was vomiting frequently as his body desperately tried to purge itself of whatever poison was making him so sick. By this time Dr. Fettes thought the situation to be "hopeless." When questioned about this at the preliminary hearing he said, "absolutely so."

Victor Christopher was crying a lot by this time, screaming sometimes, as the tumours continued to do their nefarious work. Dorothy Ramberg spoke about how each scream was like a knife passing through her body. Neither parent was getting much sleep as their son would cry in pain most of the night.

An autopsy later showed that "there was a very large tumour completely filling the right [eye socket] and extending backward along and completely destroying the nerve of the right eye." The same tumour had also destroyed the optic nerve leading to the left eye. There was also a small tumour in the left eye, but most of the damage had been done by the large one coming from the right eye.

There was nothing to help these desperate people. They could just wait for him to die, but it might be weeks or even months. No one knew.

On the evening of October 2, 1941, Victor and Dorothy Ramberg connected the exhaust pipe from their vehicle into the bedroom where the child's crib was and turned on the ignition. Dorothy later told police that, "no one could help him but his mommy and daddy . . . so we took it into our own hands." She carried her son into the bedroom, where the fumes were coming in, and held her boy until she thought he had died. Then she laid him in his bed and went out the kitchen. But she had stayed too long with the gas and collapsed once she made it back to the kitchen. She lay unconscious on the floor there for some hours. Victor had gone to turn off the motor and then went back into the bedroom, where he too was overcome by the fumes and collapsed.

Both parents eventually recovered and they were tried for murder. This had not been a suicide pact, as some of the media had initially thought. The Rambergs had been rendered unconscious by the carbon monoxide, but they had not intended for that to happen. They simply underestimated the potency of the gas. Dorothy said at one point afterwards that she had wanted to join her son, but Victor had persuaded her she needed to stay alive for the sake of her parents. Losing a grandson was hard enough for them to take without losing a daughter as well.

The trial was held on December 10 and 11, 1941. A strong defence was put forward by A. L. (Art) Smith, K.C., counsel for Dorothy Ramberg, some of which is quoted here:

> *... let us begin a new era in which decent people like [the Rambergs] will not be classed with murderers and cutthroats because they have been merciful — because they loved their child and could not bear to have him suffer . . . You are trying the first case of its kind in Canada. It is in your power to help in trying to bring about a change . . . This child was in his last illness. He was dying. His parents took the kindest means to relieve terrific suffering. Can you adjudge them guilty of murder? Would you have them hanged by the neck until dead?*
>
> *In the name of all that is decent, let us begin a new era.*

The death penalty for first-degree murder was still in effect at the time of the Rambergs' trial. It was lifted only in 1976, after over seven hundred hangings had occurred in Canada. Had they been found guilty it is likely that the Rambergs would both have been hanged.

The Rambergs' lawyers did not dispute that they had intentionally killed their child. Smith's defence was that this was not a crime but an act of human kindness. And only the jury could save them from being put to death themselves, for their act of mercy. As Art Smith said to the jury, in referring to the unsuitability of a murder charge in such a case, "It is in your power to bring about a change."

Smith's words were echoed years later in the early '80s when Henry Morgentaler was being tried in Ontario for carrying out abortions in direct violation of Canadian law at the time. His lawyer, Morris Manning, said to the jury:

> *It is up to you and you alone to apply the law to this case, and you have a right to say it shouldn't be applied.*

Morgentaler, though clearly and indisputably in violation of the law, was found not guilty, in what is known as an act of jury nullification. This is the perfectly legal right of juries to go against the law, and it resulted in a not-guilty verdict for Morgentaler. Jury nullification allows juries to refuse to come to a guilty verdict, when they believe such a verdict would be unjust, whatever the law says.

Given an understanding of their right as a jury to go against the law, as explained to the Rambergs' jury by Art Smith, who could find the Rambergs guilty? They were clearly guilty according to the law, but could anyone vote for hanging these two people who courageously acted to save their son from prolonged suffering?

During the course of the Rambergs' trial, Art Smith also made a case for the need to change Canadian law in regard to mercy killing. The law, he said, was not some permanent, fixed thing, but something that changed with conditions and times:

> *In 1832 people were hanged in England for stealing sheep. They were hanged in 1835 for stealing a letter, in 1837 for forgery and burglary, and even as late as 1861 for robbery with violence. In 1869, if I owed you $10 I could be imprisoned until I paid you.*

Smith then spoke about the fact that the country was involved in a war, where human lives were being destroyed by the thousands, while

> *we sit in this courtroom trying a man and his wife for mercifully killing a suffering, dying child in this so-called civilized age . . . We have not reached perfection in law by any means.*

J. T. Shaw, who was acting for Victor Ramberg, said that the couple did not act from a "sordid motive." He went on to say:

> *Their pitiful story touches our hearts. Here was a happy home suddenly afflicted when they knew that even the removal of both their baby's eyes would not stop his suffering and lingering death.*

After a day and a half of court proceedings the jury filed out to start their deliberations, at 1 p.m. on December 11, 1941. The judge instructed the sheriff to provide lunch for the jurors. Friends gathered around the Rambergs to comfort them. There was a very real possibility that they were headed for a death sentence. Then to everyone's astonishment there was, within minutes, a message from the jury that they had reached a decision. At 1:10 p.m. the jury was back in the courtroom.

"Have you reached a verdict?" the court clerk asked.

"Yes," the foreman answered. "Not guilty. Both of them."

* * *

It took less than ten minutes for this jury to make the decision to go against the law and refuse to convict the Rambergs.

The freeing of the Rambergs was a victory for their lawyers, especially Art Smith, and also for the idea that juries can act independently of the law — that they can go against the law and refuse to convict, if they feel such a conviction is unjust. Smith's victory in court, one might have hoped, could have led to a reconsideration of Canadian law on the issue of euthanasia. Clearly, the Ramberg's case showed, there should be a humane, legal way to deal with children in the throes of terminal agony. Adults, too, for that matter.

Smith proposed an "e-u board" in each province, consisting of three doctors and a Supreme Court judge. It would be their duty to determine, in cases like the Rambergs, if a person shall suffer no more. Shortly after Smith's appeal for consideration of an "e-u board," public awareness of the terrible actions of Hitler and the Nazis made rational discussion of the idea very difficult. Euthanasia became associated with the abhorrent ideas of racial purification and a master race. Euthanasia became, in Nazi Germany, an excuse for murdering people.

The aftermath of World War II and the revelation of the atrocities committed in the Nazi death camps profoundly affected public attitudes to the idea of assisting death. Largely because of these horrors, many decades would pass before Canada could again come to consider a legal change in the prohibition against such assistance.

GEORGE AND ELSIE DAVIS, 1942

Elsie Davis, killed by her husband on July 16, 1942, suffered from a number of ailments in her last ten years of life. Four years before she died her legs had been amputated above her knees, apparently to deal with some form of "dropsy," as they called it then, or edema, causing fluid retention in her legs. It seems an extraordinary treatment of this ailment, one that would never be used today.

Perhaps the loss of her legs was the reason Elsie became depressed and wanted to die. But she also suffered from chronic bronchitis and asthma, and she had a heart condition that probably aggravated or caused the edema. A few days before her death her doctor reported that her heartbeat had become "rapid and irregular" and that her "mental condition was not normal." He expected that she had only a short time to live. A later postmortem showed that, as well as the edema, she had a hugely enlarged heart and liver, and artery problems.

Elsie was on a constant dose of morphine and was always craving more. The drug was dutifully given to her by her loyal husband George, who for years had given his wife devoted care. He had only the amount of morphine prescribed by their doctor, and if he had given in to her wishes to have more they would eventually run short. So he had to resist her pleas for more, pleas that became particularly persistent on the night that she died.

Elsie wanted more morphine, but what she really wanted was to die. Friends testified that many times they had heard her say something like "if only God would kill me" and she often said she was going to kill herself. A few days before her death she told a friend that, "if only I could die it would be such a mercy."

George Davis was sixty-eight at the time his wife died. He had worked for many years as a baggage man for Canadian Pacific Railway, and he was a war veteran. One neighbour described him as the kindest, most patient and devoted man;

another said, "So far as I know, he never spoke a cross word to his wife." Their doctor said that, in spite of George's own heart condition, he "did a great deal of watching over her, both day and night. Since his retirement from the railroad he was with her all the time." There was also a practical nurse tending to Elsie much of the time.

On that evening of July 16, 1942, however, Elsie was particularly demanding. George told the police that, "during the evening she began begging continually for more morphine. My head got hot. I got the hammer from the porch and hit her on the head."

Apparently the weapon of the attack was actually the blunt end of a hatchet. The head injury itself was not sufficient to be the cause of death — the blow lacerated her head but did not fracture her skull. But given the parlous condition she was in, the shock of the blow was enough to kill Elsie.

George immediately phoned their doctor and asked that he come to the house. When the Doctor arrived George told him that, "I have finished her. I couldn't stand seeing her in distress any longer."

The trial began on the afternoon of Tuesday, October 7, 1942, with the Crown's case, led by D. G. Potter, ending the next day at noon. The defence team, J. L. Ross and F. Campbell, beginning after a lunch break, called no witnesses, but simply explained to the jury what had happened and why it had happened. When the defence statement was concluded later that same afternoon, the jury was sent off to conduct its deliberations.

In less than thirty minutes the jury returned with a verdict of not guilty — again an instance of jury nullification.

The presiding judge, Justice Dysart, was astonished. He said, "I thank you for your verdict, but I must express wonderment at the process by which it was reached."

The process, though, was probably a very obvious one. George Davis was technically guilty of murdering his wife. But who would want to punish him? The judge wanted the jury to follow the law, as judges do, but really he could see why the jury let Davis go. Speaking to Davis after his comment to the jury Dysart said, "You are discharged and are free to go. I think your record of many years as a kindly, faithful husband has served you in good stead and brought about this reward at the hands of the jury."

The cold and impersonal application of the law might have seen Davis hanged. As happened in the trial of the Rambergs, and in other cases to be reviewed, including that of the Inuit Eerkiyoot discussed below, a jury brought human compassion, mercy and a sense of justice to the proceedings, going beyond the limitations of the law.

EERKIYOOT, 1949

There is a tradition among some nomadic peoples of helping to end the lives of seriously ill and aged members, in order for the community to better husband its limited resources. Elders would often seek their own deaths rather than burden the community with their unproductive presence. While having respect for life, they knew that everyone had to contribute to the process of seeking food and shelter; the group could not afford to maintain those who could no longer help. This was understood and accepted; sometimes the ailing person would simply walk off into the ice and snow and eventually freeze to death. They understood that there is a time to die.

On September 10, 1949, a young Inuit man named Eerkiyoot, charged with assisting suicide, was sentenced to one year of isolation from the rest of his tribe, at the Mounted Police Detachment in Cambridge Bay, Northwest Territories. His crime was to follow the old tribal custom of helping his mother commit suicide. His forty-six-year-old mother, Nukashook, was ready to die because she had tuberculosis as well as terrible toothaches and, following tradition, she asked her son to help. Eerkiyoot tied a sealskin rope to the ridgepole of his mother's tent, put her head in a loop and pulled it tight. Nukashook died of strangulation.

The jury was sympathetic to Eerkiyoot, but was instructed by the presiding judge, A. H. Gibson, to follow the law. However, while probably not explicitly dealt with in the courtroom, and probably not mentioned or even thought of by name by the jurors, the possibility of jury nullification was clearly in play here. The jury apparently did not feel that a guilty verdict of assisting a suicide would be fair in this case, even though such a verdict would be consistent with the law.

Reluctant to punish this young man who had only followed Inuit customs and his mother's request, the jury foreman, C. J. Smith, asked if leniency could be requested — much as Robert Latimer's jury did about fifty years later. But in Eerkiyoot's case, the court was not bound by the mandatory minimum penalty that later plagued the Latimer case. Judge Gibson assured the jury members that leniency could be considered. Given that assurance the jury found Eerkiyoot guilty and he was given the token one-year sentence. He was released in six months.

In his grim task of helping his mother hang herself, Eerkiyoot had enlisted help from a cousin, Ishakak, who was tried the day after the trial of Eerkiyoot. Ishakak, although technically guilty as well, was found not guilty.

A number of additional prosecutions resulting from this clash of cultures occurred in subsequent years: notably those of Kaotok in 1955 and Amah, Avinga and Nangmalik in 1963. There were undoubtedly others but records are sketchy or nonexistent. In further examples of humane decisions, Kaotok was found not guilty and Amah, Avinga and Nangmalik were given suspended sentences.

An excellent commentary on these Inuit prosecutions was compiled by Russel Ogden and published in the magazine *Last Rights* (see Chapter Notes).

RON BROWN AND RONALD LAMBERT, 1977

In 1977, nurse's aide Ron Brown of the St. Amant Centre in Manitoba used a cotton diaper to smother eleven-year-old Ronald Lambert, who had physical and mental disabilities. The Centre is an institution that provides care to people with disabilities who do not have other options. The Lambert family placed Ronald there because they were not able to look after him. Ronald was described as being "totally dependent and tube-fed" and needing to be "strapped to his bed." Brown confessed to his superior three weeks after the deed, and advised the Executive Director of the Centre. The confession was not believed, however, and it was thought that Lambert had simply died of natural causes.

Brown was subsequently diagnosed as having acute schizophrenia, but rather than being institutionalized he was treated as an outpatient. He married in 1982, but before the marriage confessed again to his bride-to-be.

In 1995 Brown again confessed to a counsellor, after which the police finally became involved and charged him with second-degree murder. The charge was downgraded to manslaughter because, the prosecutor said, Brown "did not have the specific intent for murder." Brown could have used a psychiatric defence, based on his schizophrenia, but chose not to do so. In 1997, nineteen years after the event, he pleaded guilty

He was given two years for manslaughter, much less than the ten-year minimum he would have faced had the prosecutor held to his murder charge.

LOIS WILSON AND VICTOR HAYES, 1985

Victor Hayes was a forty-five-year-old alcoholic with various medical conditions including hepatitis, gastritis and the lingering effects of a stab wound from five years earlier. He was frequently sick. Hayes mistook his stomach condition for cancer, but an autopsy later showed it not to be so. For several weeks before his death Hayes had been pleading with his girlfriend, Lois Wilson, to help him commit suicide.

In the three years before his death in 1985, Hayes lived, from time to time, with Wilson, twenty-nine, who herself was reported to have had a personality disorder. On August 8, Hayes had been drinking heavily and asked Wilson to drive him to Ontario Place, on Lake Ontario, in Toronto. His intention was to die there. After their arrival around 11 p.m. Wilson helped Hayes take off his clothes and place them in a neat pile, and then he sat down on the edge of the dock with his feet dangling in the water below. Hayes asked Wilson, several times, to push him into the water. Finally she did give him a push from behind, and into the lake he went.

Hayes could not swim. He bobbed to the surface for a moment and Wilson tried to grab him by the arm, but failed to hold on to him. She immediately ran to inform security personnel. Later that night the police found Hayes's body.

Wilson pleaded guilty to aiding and abetting suicide and was given a six-month sentence. Prosecutor Todd Archibald said that a sentence was necessary for general deterrence because of the "sanctity of life." Judge Bruce Hawkins agreed. However, the sentence was much less that the maximum allowed by law, which was fourteen years.

This was one of the first convictions in Canada for aiding and abetting suicide, the earlier ones, cited above, having occurred in the Northwest Territories and involving Inuit men and traditional practices of assisting suicide.

NANCY B, 1992

A twenty-five-year-old woman, known in the literature only as Nancy B, had been suffering for two and a half years from Guillain-Barré syndrome, a disabling neurological condition. By late 1991 she was confined to Hôtel Dieu de Québec, a teaching hospital in Quebec City where she was kept alive by mechanical respiratory support. She was completely immobile and would be confined, as long as she lived, to her bed. She could not breathe without the respirator and would quickly die if disconnected from it. But she could go on indefinitely with it. Her mind was not affected by the disease, but she was faced with the prospect of spending the rest of her time, which could have been years, without being able to move from her bed.

Nancy applied for an injunction to require the hospital and her doctor to comply with her wish to be disconnected so she could die. She wished to have the breathing support removed so she could just die a natural death. Preferably, she would also be given drugs by her doctor to put her in a deep sleep so she would be unaware of the sensation of suffocation.

Judge Dufour of the Quebec Superior Court ruled that the mechanical intervention could be stopped, and that her doctor and the hospital could provide "the necessary assistance in circumstances such as these, so that everything can take place in a manner respecting the dignity of the plaintiff." This meant not only that the patient had the full right to have treatment stopped but that her doctor would not be liable for homicide or assisted suicide, including for the action of preparing the patient for death by inducing a deep sleep.

Any patient has the right to refuse treatment, but the tricky part here was in allowing the doctor to induce the deep sleep, an action that could previously be seen as assisting suicide. In that respect, then, this was an important precedent. However, since this case was defined as neither a homicide nor a suicide, but a natural death, it did not have a direct impact on the issue of physician-assisted suicide or euthanasia, although it was widely seen as moving closer to legalization of at least the former.

JEAN AND CECIL BRUSH, 1994

Jean and Cecil Brush, of Stoney Creek, Ontario, were happily married for fifty-eight years when Cecil began to have very serious health problems. By 1994, when he had reached the age of eighty-one, he had lost most of his eyesight and was suffering from Alzheimer's and depression. Jean, who was year or so younger, was finding the situation very difficult to manage. He told her repeatedly that he wanted to die, preferably in his sleep. Finally Jean tried to end both of their lives by giving him and then herself a large number of sleeping pills. They fell unconscious but were found while still alive and both woke in the hospital.

Some months later Cecil was admitted to a nursing home. While he was there Jean picked him up, supposedly to take him to lunch, but instead took him to their house where they both lay down on some blankets and she stabbed him several times in the stomach and then did the same to herself. Later that afternoon their daughter Joan came by their house and discovered them, lying in blood on the blankets, holding hands. This time he died, but again she survived. She was charged with manslaughter.

Jean had written a heartbreaking suicide note:

> *Cec's and my situation is getting worse day by day and will not get better. Cec being blind and with Alzheimer's disease is like being in a nightmarish hell. We have lived our lifetime and it must end before we become vegetables. Medical profession and Governments won't do anything to use euthanasia or mercy killing to put suffering elderly people out of the torture and agony that they are in.*
>
> *People in nursing homes, the people in psychiatric wards, mentally and physically dead but breathing and they are kept alive as long as possible. Why? Why? Handicapped children, extremely handicapped in mental incapabilities and physical incapabilities kept alive but not living per se.*
>
> *Do the medical profession and Governments care what effect this has on the families? It doesn't seem like it.*
>
> *Joan's life is being disrupted and it will get worse for her and that sacrifice shouldn't be asked of anyone. Families have their own lives to consider. Life for the young must go on.*

Cec as he was, young, vibrant, full of life is no more. He is a shell, dead but not buried because he still breathes.

Darling Joan: No matter how it happens, it's going to be a shock. I can't let Dad suffer any more. I know I have to go also. I transferred Dad's small account to the joint account but Dana Kelly needs a copy of the Power of Attorney — namely Dad's. Would you take it to her when you have a chance and time?

We love you and Karen and Shawn and adding Michael to the family.

Jean pleaded guilty to manslaughter and was given a suspended sentence and eighteen months probation. The judge wrote:

Considering the totality of everything presented to me, I find that in this case exceptional circumstances exist which justify the imposition of a non-custodial sentence. There is no doubt in my mind on what has been presented to me that imposing the most lenient sentence possible would serve the ends of justice and that Mrs. Brush remaining in the community would not endanger the safety of the community.

I can see no principle of sentencing which would cause me to incarcerate Jean Brush and perhaps shorten her life. She has already suffered a harsher sentence than could ever be imposed by this Court, the loss of her loving and devoted husband under these tragic circumstances and the trauma of becoming involved in a very public criminal prosecution at this stage of her life.

I will not compound this tragedy by incarcerating Jean Brush. Accordingly, I am suspending the passing of sentence and Jean Brush is placed on probation for a period of eighteen months. The probation order will contain the usual statutory terms . . .

Note the role of prosecutorial discretion shown in this case. Technically, what Jean Brush did was first-degree murder with a mandatory minimum sentence of twenty-five years in prison. Second-degree murder has a mandatory minimum of ten years. The manslaughter charge, though, allowed full judicial discretion in sentencing, the importance of which can be seen in this case.

* * *

In all of these examples we see deaths caused by acts of mercy, and we see mercy shown to those who caused the deaths. In none of these cases was the full force of the law applied to the perpetrators of the supposed crimes. These serve as examples of a changing public attitude to assisted death — that at times it would seem, whatever the law says, morally wrong to allow suffering to go on unabated, and unjust to punish too severely those who help those who are suffering too severely.

The direction was not always forward, however. There were some serious setbacks in the movement to a more progressive law on assisted death.

CHAPTER 2
ROBERT LATIMER: JUSTICE GOES AWRY — 1993

The Robert Latimer story was one of the most widely covered news stories in Canadian history. It is a story, unlike some of the previous ones, where the justice system found no way of mitigating the prescribed legal punishment for what was essentially an act of mercy.

In 1993 Latimer ended his twelve-year-old daughter Tracy's suffering from the ravages of severe cerebral palsy. For this "crime" he went through seven years of legal proceedings, was found guilty of second-degree murder, spent seven years (2000 to 2007) in prison and another three on day parole. In 2010 he was finally released, but he remains on parole for life. He continues to be in the news because of restrictions that were subsequently placed on him by the Parole Board of Canada.

Latimer was the object of much hostility from

organizations opposed to any form of assisted or hastened death. This included the Catholic Church, the Euthanasia Prevention Coalition (EPC) and other such organizations. However, such hostility was not shown by most Canadians. There was widespread public sympathy for Latimer — his action in ending the life of his daughter was generally seen as a courageous act of mercy.

LATIMER'S MOTIVATION

When Robert Latimer ended the life of his suffering daughter in November 1993, he had previously given her almost thirteen years of dedicated care. Tracy had been born with severe brain damage, probably as a result of a faulty heart monitor in the hospital, and she never had any chance of anything resembling a normal life. Both her mental capacities and her muscle control were severely compromised. Doctors estimated that she never exceeded the mental capacity of a three- to four-month-old baby. By all accounts of people who knew them, the Latimers loved their daughter and could cope with her mental disability, but they became increasingly distraught by the physical suffering Tracy was enduring. At the same time, for medical reasons, Tracy was never able to take any pain reliever stronger than Tylenol No. 2. Tracy's spastic, uncontrolled body movements caused great damage to her frail body, and she developed debilitating conditions such as severe curvature of her spine.

Tracy underwent a series of corrective operations but continued to deteriorate. Her hip joints often became dislocated due to her body movements, causing her to scream out in pain. As she approached her thirteenth birthday her orthopedic surgeon decided that Tracy's femurs would have to be cut off and the painful hip joints removed. Both hips could not be done at the same time; there would need to be about a one-year gap between them. Each of these operations would entail a considerable new and lengthy period of pain.

The Latimers were distraught by this proposal; they had thought that Tracy's problematic hip joints could be repaired, not just removed. They felt that the proposed operation would be mutilation of their daughter and the resulting pain would be further torture for her. "Maybe it's time to call Dr. Kevorkian," Laura Latimer said to her husband, not literally meaning it, but expressing how she felt about Tracy's condition. It seemed quite clear to everyone involved that Tracy would be better off dead. Robert apparently said nothing in response to his wife's comment, but the idea was planted in his mind. He decided that it was his responsibility to do this thing for Tracy.

On his own, on Sunday October 24, 1993, just before the new operation was scheduled and while the rest of his family was at church, Robert Latimer ended Tracy's life with carbon monoxide poisoning. When Laura returned and found the body of her daughter, not knowing that Robert had done it, she said, "Finally Tracy got a break."

Latimer's decision to do what he did was not the wisest of choices, but there is little doubt that it was a compassionate one. As he has repeatedly said over the years, "It was the best thing for Tracy." And no doubt it was. The trouble was that it was not the best thing for Robert or his family. It need not have been so bad, but the legal system could not find a way to treat this case with the same sense of mercy and compassion that Latimer had shown for his daughter. Fifty years earlier the Rambergs had similarly ended the agony of their son, using carbon monoxide, but they paid no additional penalty as their jury refused to punish them for their act of mercy.

For various reasons that I will touch on below, Latimer paid a very heavy price indeed for his act of mercy. There is no evidence whatsoever in support of the claims that this was something other than an act of mercy — that a selfish Latimer just wanted to get this disabled child off his hands, or other unwarranted and unjustified charges that have been made against him. His judge and jury, who had heard all of the evidence, had no doubt that this was an act of compassion. Even his prosecutor allowed that it could well have been so. (See Chapter Notes for more on Latimer's character.)

Would a self-serving person risk so much to help his child? She probably would have died soon anyway. But to Latimer it was wrong let her suffering go on any longer. Wise? Maybe not. Compassionate and merciful? Definitely.

WHAT WENT WRONG, PART 1: THE INVESTIGATION

Latimer was immediately a suspect in the death of his daughter and was interrogated by the police. He is not by nature a manipulative or deceptive person, and when asked several times by the police if he wanted a lawyer he unwisely declined.

Soon he was revealing everything to the police, without the aid of a lawyer, and he ended up compromising his subsequent defence. Eventually Latimer did of course get a defence lawyer, Mark Brayford, who immediately tried to get the uncounselled testimony of his client removed from the record. This request was refused and the prosecution had its way with all of that unguarded testimony.

The problem here was that Latimer is not a man designed

to handle legal situations like this; he is not sophisticated in legal matters. He did not feel he was a criminal and could not, initially, see the need for a lawyer. Anyone with any real experience with the law, or anyone with a guilty conscience, would have realized immediately that one should consult with legal counsel before admitting to anything. But Latimer had neither legal experience nor a guilty conscience. He believed then as he does now that he did the right thing for Tracy.

The police, knowing what could be in store for Latimer, and some of whom were his friends, should have insisted, not just asked, that he seek counsel at an early point in the interrogation.

WHAT WENT WRONG, PART 2: THE FIRST PROSECUTOR

When Latimer first went to court he was faced with a very aggressive and hostile prosecutor, Randy Kirkham, who insisted on charging Latimer with murder. Kirkham could have opted for manslaughter, a charge that would have allowed for some flexibility in the sentencing of Latimer. But murder has little flexibility. When Latimer was found guilty, he had to be given the mandatory minimum penalty for murder: life with ten years before full parole. The initial charge, then, became the direct cause of Latimer's lengthy prison sentence.

Kirkham expressed undue hostility to Latimer in other ways as well. He collaborated with the RCMP in screening prospective jurors for the trial, which, when discovered (by accident) was regarded by the Supreme Court of Canada as sufficient reason to throw out the entire first trial. Hence a second trial.

Kirkham's venomous attitude toward Latimer was

revealed in some of his statements in court. At one point he described Latimer as:

> . . . *foul, callous, cold, calculating and not motivated by anything other than making his own life easier.*

Kirkham was later admonished by the Saskatchewan Court of Appeal for such intemperate comments, comments that were contrary to what was said about Latimer by all who knew him.

WHAT WENT WRONG, PART 3: THE SECOND TRIAL

The second trial began innocently enough with a new judge and a new, more reasonable prosecutor, and this time with no jury-fixing. The new prosecutor even allowed that an action like Latimer's can be taken out of love, not malice. But it is still illegal, he argued, and therefore Latimer should still be found guilty.

Unfortunately, because this was a retrial, the prosecutor did not have the option of reducing the charge to manslaughter, something he might well have done. The charge in a retrial must be the same as in the original trial. Once again, then, Latimer was charged with second-degree murder.

There was an important, little-known but long-standing legal principle at play in this trial, as there is in many trials where a law has been broken but the jury is sympathetic to the defendant. The principle, mentioned in Chapter 1, is that juries have the right to full independence in coming to their verdict, no matter what the law says should happen. When juries go against the law it is called jury nullification.

As also mentioned in Chapter 1, this principle had been

used to good effect in the trials of Henry Morgentaler in the 1970s and '80s. Morgentaler openly carried out abortions in defiance of the law and was repeatedly prosecuted, but all four of his juries refused to find him guilty. It was obvious that banning abortion was not supported by public opinion, so in 1988 the Supreme Court of Canada struck down the abortion law. This, one might think, was a great triumph not just for Morgentaler and his lawyer, Morris Manning, but also for the Canadian justice system, a triumph brought about by juries trumping a law that was not in accord with community standards of justice.

The trouble is that, in spite of this triumph of justice over blindly following the law, the Supreme Court decided that it was "troubled" by what had happened, and banned the future use of the sort of defence Manning had used for Morgentaler (and Art Smith had used for the Rambergs) — telling the jury that it was up to them and them alone to decide if the law was to be applied in that case. The Court could not very well have banned jury nullification itself, since jury independence is a cornerstone of our legal system and banning it would seriously change the nature of our judicial process. But the Court banned mentioning of it to juries. So now juries can still practice nullification, but no one can tell them about it.

As a result of this odd Supreme Court directive, juries now cannot be told that they have the right to go against the law. This became a very important factor in the Latimer trial. His jury was very sympathetic and did not want to mete out a heavy penalty for what he had done, but they thought they were obliged to find him guilty. With defence lawyer Brayford having to keep silent about this, and with the prosecutor and judge in effect telling the jury that the law demanded a guilty verdict, it is not surprising that they did find Latimer guilty. They thought they had no choice.

There is more to this story. The jury, while not understanding their right to nullify, was clearly toying with the idea anyway, or at least trying to find a way to lessen the penalty. They did not want a severe penalty, so they asked the judge that, if they found Latimer guilty, could they have a say in the sentencing? The judge said yes, that was possible, but neglected to tell them that murder entailed the mandatory minimum penalty of ten years. They could negotiate the sentence, all right, but only for possible imprisonment of over ten years.

The jury was stunned when this process played out — when they discovered what their guilty verdict entailed. Some of them cried. They felt betrayed. In desperation the jury asked that a special exemption be made in this case, and that Latimer be given only a year in prison. The judge agreed to try this, but as expected it was overturned on appeal. And Latimer went on to serve his ten years.

There were two points in the trials at which this fate for Latimer could have been avoided. One was when the charge of murder was established in the first trial by prosecutor Kirkham; as mentioned earlier, if he had laid a charge of manslaughter instead, then a guilty verdict would have allowed flexibility in sentencing — one year would have been possible.

The one other point in the trials when the severe penalty could have been avoided — the only other point — was when the jury gave its verdict. Once they said "guilty" the thing was done, out of their hands, out of even the judge's hands, because of the mandatory minimum.

Had Brayford been able to speak to the jury openly, as

Morris Manning had years ago in the Morgentaler trials, this jury might well have found Latimer not guilty. Had the jury just known about the mandatory minimum, they might similarly have refused to find him guilty. But Brayford could not inform the jury of its rights, and the judge refused to tell the jury of the severity of the impending penalty. And Latimer became the victim of these circumstances.

All of this was appealed to the Supreme Court of Canada, but because no mistakes in law had been made the Supreme Court judges refused to intervene. The sentence was certainly unjust, and even some of the Supreme Court justices appeared to understand that, but they felt unable to give a more just legal resolution. They recommended that Latimer seek clemency, but for various reasons that turned out not to be a viable option.

WHAT WENT WRONG, PART 4: THE PRISON

Coinciding with the start of Latimer's prison sentence, starting in January 2000, Canadian Solicitor General Lawrence MacAulay issued an unusual edict that persons who were convicted for murder of any kind had to spend the first two years of their sentence in a maximum-security prison. This was contrary to the normal procedure of allowing prison officials discretion to assess new prisoners and determine where they would best fit into the system. It was ludicrous to think that the mild-mannered Latimer would need to go to maximum-security, but MacAulay made it mandatory. Was this an intentional slap directed at Latimer? It certainly looks like it was. MacAulay has been a lifetime supporter of the "pro-life" movement. To many people his edict seemed like a gratuitous, petty and vindictive action against Latimer.

Latimer did go to maximum-security prison for seven

months, but then MacAulay's edict was forgotten, the prison system's normal procedures were re-established, and Latimer was relocated to a more suitable lower-security prison.

Latimer did not have an easy time of it, especially in high security where he was in the company of many very violent criminals, but he survived it. When I was giving a public lecture on the Latimer story in Kamloops, B.C., in 2011, a rough-looking man entered the lecture hall and then walked in and out several times while I was speaking. As soon as the floor was opened to questions, he yelled out:

"I was in prison with Latimer; we wanted to kill him, and it's too bad we didn't." Then he stomped out, but kept peering in through a window in the back of the hall. I left protectively surrounded by a phalanx of those who had hosted the talk.

MacAulay has been a longtime member of the Liberal Party as a Member of Parliament from Prince Edward Island. In July 2014 he announced that he planned to vote pro-life if the abortion issue ever came back to Parliament. He changed his mind only after Party Leader Justin Trudeau said that all Liberal candidates in the next election would vote pro-choice.

Twice I wrote to MacAulay to ask him about the directive he had issued that resulted in Latimer going to a maximum-security prison, but I never had an answer.

WHAT WENT WRONG, PART 5: THE PAROLE BOARD

Latimer was convicted partly on the evidence he gave before consulting a lawyer; he was charged with murder rather than manslaughter; his first trial was thrown out because of jury-fixing; his second trial involved his sympathetic jurors not being fully informed; the one-year token sentence that his jurors and his judge all wanted him to have was disallowed by the Appeal Court and the Supreme Court of Canada; he was initially sent to a high-security prison where his life was probably in danger; and he was held in prison for seven years before being eligible for day parole. So now, surely, he would be granted day parole and this persecution of Robert Latimer would come to an end.

Latimer's first parole hearing was in December 2007. He was eligible then for day parole, which he would have to serve for three years before being out on full parole. After the repeated and extended punishments and humiliations he had already been through, surely the parole hearing would be a formality. Surely this sorry chapter in the administration of justice in Canada would now quietly end.

But it did not end. The three-person Parole Board (all political appointees) viciously attacked Latimer, seemed to regard him as a danger to society, and refused parole.

Afterwards, Latimer seemed resigned to his fate — by this time he was very cynical about the justice system and expected nothing positive from it. However, John Dixon, of the B.C. Civil Liberties Association, took up Latimer's cause and he persuaded a colleague at the Association, Vancouver lawyer Jason Gratl, to launch an appeal. Gratl did this at his own expense.

Gratl's powerfully worded appeal overcame odds of about a thousand to one against parole reversals, and the Parole Board's appeal body (consisting of lawyers rather than political appointees) overturned the denial of Latimer's day parole. Finally Latimer, like his daughter Tracy, got a break.

But still this was not the end of Latimer's travails. While on three years of day parole, during which time he was required to spend most nights in a "half-way" house, he was under close scrutiny by the Board, and subjected to what appeared to be gratuitous harassment, as though he was some sort of dangerous threat to the public. Latimer had studied to become an electrician while in prison and through a friend I was able to get him apprentice work with a Victoria electrician. The Parole Board allowed this, but insisted that Latimer had to phone into the Board office from every stop he and the electrician made in the course of a day's work, even if it was just for coffee.

Among the many other restrictions placed on Latimer by the Parole Board, one seems particularly ironic. Latimer's nephew, quadriplegic Don Danbrook, who lived in Vancouver, often came to visit Latimer in prison; they were quite close. Travelling was not so easy for Danbrook, and when Latimer was released on day parole Danbrook asked if Latimer could come to visit him at his home in Vancouver. Latimer applied for permission to do this (his travel on day parole was restricted to a very limited distance from his half-way house in downtown Victoria). The Board turned him down, in part on the grounds that he was not allowed to be in the company of a handicapped person.

* * *

After three years of day parole Latimer was granted full parole. But this was not an end to Parole Board restrictions. A murder conviction entails a life sentence, which means parole for life. Just a few months before this book was written he was refused permission to visit South America, because the Board could not be sure that he could be trusted if unsupervised. Eventually this decision was also overturned on appeal.

Canadians do not generally support the right to carry out, with impunity, acts of involuntary euthanasia such as what Latimer did for Tracy; that is still viewed as highly problematic and risky. But the Latimer affair, and in particular the untoward severity of his punishment, has helped raise public awareness of the inadequacies and inflexibility of Canadian laws in regard to compassionate assistance in ending of life.

CHAPTER 3
SUE RODRIGUEZ: WHO OWNS MY LIFE? — 1993

A landmark event in the history of the movement to legalize assisted death in Canada began with a videotaped statement issued to a parliamentary committee in 1992. In November of that year, a severely ill Victoria woman, Sue Rodriguez, issued the video statement, in which she made a moving plea for the legal right to get assistance in dying:

> If I cannot give consent to my own death, whose body is this? Who owns my body? Who owns my life?

The Rodriguez case, like the Latimer case and the Martens case described in Chapter 5, captured the imagination of the Canadian public, and brought national attention to the issue of finding more humane approaches to dying in Canada.

Suffering from amyotrophic lateral sclerosis (ALS, also known as Lou Gehrig's disease), but loving life and her young son, Sue Rodriguez wanted to keep living as long as possible before she became completely paralyzed. ALS is a progressive muscle disorder that slowly takes away all conscious bodily control, eventually leaving a perfectly intact mind trapped inside an immobile body. Rodriguez wanted to live, but not past that point of becoming completely trapped. The trouble was, when she reached that point she would no longer be able to take her own life. She would need help. But giving help would be illegal, according to Section 241(b) of the *Criminal Code of Canada*, which prohibited anyone else from assisting her to end her life.

Rodriguez died on February 12, 1994, in the company of politician Svend Robinson, who at the time was an NDP Member of Parliament for Burnaby, B.C., and a supporter of the right-to-die movement. Also present, reportedly, was an unidentified doctor who supposedly helped carry out the procedure that ended her life. Sue apparently took a lethal dose of the drug secobarbital, although this was not entirely clear. Robinson says that he lay down with her as she died and held her in his arms. "It took a very long time for her heart to stop beating," he said.

But who administered the drug to her? She was far too disabled by this time to have done it herself. It seems unlikely that Robinson himself would have taken such a chance. Did the mysterious doctor, whose identity has never been revealed, risk his or her career and do it, as is commonly assumed?

It seems that someone risked his or her future to administer a lethal drug to the desperately ill Sue Rodriguez, but this courageous act has gone entirely unrecognized, because the person who did it could, if recognized, be prosecuted. Robinson has stated that he will never reveal who it was.

*   *   *

Born in Winnipeg in 1950, Sue Shipley, later Rodriguez, grew up in the Toronto suburb of Thornhill. She was an active girl, taking ballet and music lessons, enjoying outdoor activities and the social side of school. Although she wasn't a great student, Sue was good-natured and had lots of friends. In high school she helped out in her mother's nursery school and then decided to take early childhood education at college, but did not stick with that. At the age of twenty-one she began teaching exercise classes for adults, and became Sue Hendricks in a short-lived marriage. In 1974 she began work as a secretary in the Outdoor Recreation Department of Seneca College in Willowdale near Toronto, where as a staff member she was able to participate in many of the outdoor programs, which she loved.

In 1976 Sue decided to do something completely different and moved to San Diego, where she could enjoy the warm weather and still drive to the Sierra Nevada mountains for cross-country skiing. She took up photography and did freelance work for a few years, and was in every respect a very active, healthy young woman.

In 1980 Sue married young biochemist Henry Rodriguez. They moved to San Francisco, where she found work as a program assistant at Stanford University. Their only child, Cole, was born in 1984 when she was thirty-three. However, by 1988, when the family moved to a large house just outside Victoria, the marriage was troubled, and Sue had difficulty finding a job. Finally she did get some work in a real estate firm, but it went bankrupt in February of 1991. That same month Henry left home. And then, still in February, she began to notice an odd sensation and weakness in her left hand.

Her symptoms slowly became worse and in August of 1991, just after she had turned forty-one, she was diagnosed as having ALS. The disease is incurable and Sue was given two to three years to live. Some live longer — Stephen Hawking has lived over fifty years with a version of the disease. Sue hoped to be among such outliers but, as it turned out, she was not.

The disease is a grim and relentless one. It cannot be resisted, or at least no one knows how to do that. It just proceeds on its own schedule, steadily destroying the motor neurons that control the body's muscles. The muscles then begin to shrink and stiffen. Progressive difficulties in speaking, swallowing, smiling and breathing ensue. Cruelly, the senses and one's mental capacity remain intact as the body stops working. Death usually comes from respiratory failure.

Sue later discovered that modern medicine could keep her alive for a longer period than the few years that had been predicted for her. She could be put in a machine to keep her breathing and food could be funnelled into her stomach to avoid the problem with swallowing. Her mind would remain acute, but it would be trapped in a non-functioning body. Some people might want to live on like that as long as possible. Sue Rodriguez did not.

* * *

At the same time Sue was struggling with the reality of what was going to happen to her body, she was having to deal with taking care of her seven-year-old son and with finding money to live on. Mercifully, her estranged husband Henry, when he heard of her affliction, returned home to pay the bills and take care of the declining woman and their son.

In trying to cope with the disease, Sue read what she could about it and attended a chapter of the ALS Society in Victoria. She did not find the experience comforting. As one supporter described it, what she had to look forward to was becoming a "helpless, drooling, physically-atrophied captive of this disease, totally dependent on others and machines for an ever-attenuated form of mere biological existence." Sue did not want to live that way.

But for ALS sufferers, Canada offered nothing else but that hellish possibility. Some might die relatively soon and find relief that way. Some, like Stephen Hawking, might have a less debilitating strain of the illness and be able to continue on with some degree of control and to engage in some semblance of a normal life. But others, like Sue, face a lingering period of being trapped in their helpless bodies.

While contemplating her difficult future, Sue read the famous book *Final Exit* by American Derek Humphry and was much relieved to see that there could be another way out. Maybe she would end her life quickly and painlessly at a time of her choosing. Except that her doctor could not and would not help her. He told her about hospice care, which she thought that was "fine for people with other forms of illness, especially cancers that require pain management." But the comprehensive misery of ALS could not be relieved by hospice procedures. The pain and discomfort of other diseases can sometimes be lessened by health care techniques, but there is no effective way to mitigate the devastating effects of total paralysis.

Another doctor she consulted was no more help, telling her that, "I'd like to help you but legally my hands are tied."

By May of 1992, only eight months after her initial diagnosis, Sue had lost the use of both hands and was finding it hard to walk. She had considerable difficulty swallowing, already making the possibility of taking barbiturates to end her life problematic, without assistance. She could not, even at this early stage, end her own life. If ALS sufferers are to end their own lives, without assistance, they must do so at the onset of the disease. Otherwise it will soon be too late.

Suicide, Sue's great hope, was rapidly disappearing as an option. And no one seemed to be willing to assist her. She attended a meeting in Victoria held by the Toronto-based Dying with Dignity Society. Although they could not give her the sort of assistance she wanted, they did give her the number of the Right to Die Society of Canada. It took her several weeks to follow up on this because she found all of these efforts exhausting.

Finally in August 1992, she arranged a meeting with John Hofsess, founder of the organization, who, unlike those she had previously approached, was immediately willing to offer his help. In fact, Hofsess not only agreed to do whatever he could to assist her, he made an extraordinary pledge that he published in his magazine *Last Rights*:

> *I, John Hofsess, do agree to assist Sue Rodriguez in terminating her life at a time of her choosing, preferably by permission of Canadian law but failing that, by the moral authority of personal conscience.*

Hofsess pledged to break the law, if he could not get the law changed, thus setting himself up for prosecution for assisted suicide, with the possibility of a fourteen-year prison sentence. He might even be held liable for murder, depending on the details of what actually took place. If Rodriguez could actually carry out the final act herself, say by taking some pills that Hofsess handed her, then that would be construed as assisted suicide. But if Hofsess had to put the pills directly into her mouth then that could be considered murder, since the final action would not have been taken by the dying person.

By Hofsess's account, he told Sue that it was

> . . . *time that suicide came out of the closet. We have two options: we can sneak around in guilt-ridden secrecy trying to devise a way for you to die and hope that my involvement in your death never comes to light. Or we can break the silence once and for all. Instead of seeing ourselves as powerless, as do so many of the elderly and ill, we can at least possess the power of honesty. We can state publicly that there is nothing to be ashamed of that a person with a terminal illness wants to die, and due to various disabilities needs help in carrying out her wishes. We can ask for a court ruling as to whether you have any rights as a disabled person to terminate your life with assistance.*

Hofsess planned to raise funds, get legal assistance and try to get the courts to change the law. He wondered if there might be some other country where Sue could go to get assistance in dying, but at that time there was none. If all else failed, he said, "Whatever Sue Rodriguez needs from me will be given and *will* be done." His pledge, he was saying, would stand, whatever happened with the law.

* * *

Hofsess was neither a lawyer nor a legal expert, and he needed help in preparing a case to take to the courts. The general idea was clear to him: it was unfair that someone could legally attempt to commit suicide, but a severely disabled person could not get assistance to do what an able-bodied person could do. To prepare the argument in detail, Hofsess approached Eike-Henner Kluge, a philosopher at the University of Victoria. Kluge had been and continues to be a key Canadian spokesperson on end-of-life matters. Some biographical details of this remarkable and influential man, who appears frequently in this book, are given in Chapter 12.

In early 1993, Kluge prepared on behalf of Sue Rodriguez a legal argument for overturning the law prohibiting assisted suicide, and Victoria lawyer Chris Considine was engaged to bring the case forward to the B.C. Supreme Court. There it was rejected. Then the case went to the B.C. Court of Appeals, where it was also rejected. Finally it was taken to the Supreme Court of Canada (SCC) where, on September 30, 1993, it was rejected by a vote of five to four. This tantalizingly close vote has meant that thousands of Canadians have endured prolonged and unwanted suffering in the past twenty years.

What exactly was the case and why was it rejected?

The assisted suicide law was challenged on the grounds that it violated certain sections of the *Canadian Charter of*

Rights and Freedoms, passed by Parliament in 1982. Since the *Charter* was passed the Supreme Court's role has greatly expanded, as now it is charged with determining whether or not existing laws are in accord with the *Charter*. The SCC can overturn any law it considers to be in violation of the *Charter*.

Some limits, however, are placed on the Court at the beginning of the *Charter*; the very first section specifies that the rights and freedoms guaranteed by the *Charter* are subject to *"reasonable limits"* that "can be demonstrably justified in a free and democratic society."

This means that a law can be demonstrably unconstitutional — it can violate the *Charter* — but still be allowed by the Court because some strong reason can be put forth for retaining it. This would prove to be a key consideration in the Rodriguez judgment.

The most powerful argument used at the time to support the Rodriguez case was based on Section 15 of the *Charter*, which states that "every individual is equal under the law and has the right to the equal protection and equal benefit of the law without discrimination." In particular that discrimination cannot be based on "race, national or ethnic origin, colour, religion, sex, age, or mental or *physical disability*" (emphasis added).

The case here was simple and clear: Suicide is legal and is available to able-bodied people. Rodriguez, when she became sufficiently disabled, would require assistance in carrying out this legal act. Being denied such assistance, then, and being denied a right that able-bodied people have, was discriminatory. This is clearly in violation of Section 15, and the case would probably have been won by Rodriguez — except for Section 1 of the *Charter*, the "reasonable limits" clause.

Justice John Sopinka wrote the judgment for the slim majority on the Court. He allowed that prohibiting assisted suicide for someone like Sue Rodriguez could be considered to be discriminatory and a violation of Section 15 of the *Charter*, although he did not go quite so far as to say that it was so. The trouble, in Sopinka's estimation, was that any concern about discrimination in Section 15 should be over-ridden by Section 1, because of "justifiable" worry about misuse of assisted suicide if the prohibition were lifted. It may be discrimination against Sue Rodriguez, Sopinka was saying, but greater harm would come from allowing assisted suicide. His concern, shared by many others at the time, was that certain disadvantaged people, including the elderly, would be subject to being done in by unscrupulous people seeking some personal advantage — say, inheriting money or getting rid of a bothersome need to offer care.

So, whatever the case about discrimination, Sopinka and the Supreme Court majority in this case found that retaining the law on assisted suicide constituted a "reasonable limit" on what we should regard as discrimination.

The Supreme Court decision cited no actual examples of the abuse the judges feared. In fact, the rarity of convictions for assisted suicide (see Appendix 1), and the compelling and sympathetic circumstances of those who were prosecuted, strongly suggested that there would not be wanton abuse if legalization of assisted suicide, under restricted conditions, were to be allowed. Moreover, although there were at the time no countries with statutes legalizing assisted suicide, it was not a criminal offence in France and Germany, and there had been no wave of abuses in those countries. On the whole, it seemed to many reasonable observers that the blanket prohibition, even that relatively early date in 1993, was too far-reaching and unnecessary. To the Supreme Court majority, though, it seemed that the idea of discrimination in the *Charter,* not the law on assisted suicide, was too far-reaching.

The decision also made much of the supposed critical difference between active and passive forms of euthanasia — that the former, needed by Rodriguez (who wanted to die only after she had become completely paralyzed), was reprehensible while the latter was perfectly permissible.

Justice Sopinka's position, in part at least, seemed to arise from his strongly held belief in the "sanctity of life." In his ruling he claimed that *"the active participation by one individual in the death of another is intrinsically morally and legally wrong."*

Is this view — that that taking the life of another person is "intrinsically morally wrong" — a sound one? It certainly could be argued that it is *generally* morally wrong, but *intrinsically morally wrong* means that it is by nature wrong and therefore always wrong. The Catholic Church takes this position based upon the idea of "the supreme ownership of God over the lives of His creatures." By this reckoning it is up to God, and only God, to end a life, because all lives belong to Him. This leads to certain logical inconsistencies that are dealt with in various ways.

However, whatever the merits of or flaws in the court's reasoning, this ruling stood for over two decades as the final word on assisted suicide.

* * *

It is often argued that 1993 was too early for the assisted suicide law to be struck down, and, given the information available at the time, it probably was. *Charter* challenges were relatively new and the meaning of some of the sections of the *Charter* were still being worked out. Also, in 1993 no other countries had as yet formulated permissive end-of-life legislation; by 2015 such legislation had not only become widespread but also clearly illustrated that the fears of the Supreme Court majority — that removing the prohibition on assisted suicide would open the door to unscrupulous behavior — were not valid.

It certainly is much easier now to make a case for striking down the prohibition of assisted suicide than it was twenty years ago. Yet one still wonders if the case could have been won back then, and that the additional years of suffering could have been avoided. It was, even then, a very close vote; if one Supreme Court justice had changed his or her mind, the case would have been won then, in 1993.

Lawyer Chris Considine, acting for Sue Rodriguez, made his presentation to the Supreme Court on May 20, 1993. All nine members of the Court were there, led by Chief Justice Antonio Lamer. There were four other speakers (interveners) on behalf of Sue Rodriguez, including Hofsess's Right to Die Society, represented by lawyers John Laskin and Robyn Bell. Lawyers on behalf of the Attorneys General of B.C. and Canada and then three interveners representing pro-life organizations, including the Canadian Conference of Catholic Bishops, spoke against Rodriguez.

In studying the arguments used in the hearing in detail, and recognizing Justice Sopinka's strong personal views about the sanctity of life, it seems unlikely that anything could have won that day. Considine did come very close to winning, and it could well be that any of the alternative strategies suggested above would have lost votes, not gained them. Or have had no impact at all.

It is also quite likely that even if one vote had been changed it would have simply allowed this one case to proceed: only a constitutional exemption would be made for Sue Rodriguez, allowing assistance in dying in this one case, but the law prohibiting assisted suicide would remain in place. That was all Considine was asking. So a change in the law was probably much farther away than that one vote. In fact, it took over twenty more years.

* * *

What of John Hofsess, who was so prominent in the early stages of the Rodriguez case? In early March of 1993, as planning for the court presentations was proceeding, an odd event took place. A few weeks earlier Hofsses had announced publicly that more than one doctor and at least two spectators would attend and assist the death of Sue Rodriguez, whenever she decided was the time for her to die.

Hofsess said that the event would be a public one with himself, politician Svend Robinson and possibly a number of other people present: "the more people present the stronger the message that is sent to the government." Almost immediately, however, on March 16, Rodriguez issued a statement that Hofsess had acted without her permission. She wrote:

> *I deeply regret that John has made statements concerning my life which are both inaccurate and made without consultation with me . . . I am seeking the right to die with dignity and certainly not in the public eye.*

After the March 16 incident she and Svend Robinson

announced that they were going to sever all ties with Hofsess's Right to Die organization and that in future Robinson would act as her media spokesperson and fundraiser. Robinson spoke of Hofsess's action as an "error in judgment." Robinson replaced Hofsess as the main public figure in the Rodriguez case, just as Considine replaced Eike-Henner Kluge as the main legal strategist.

That is why it was Svend Robinson, and not John Hofsess, who was with Sue when she died, even though Hofsess had been the first to give Rodriguez any hope that she might be able to receive assistance in dying. And, more than that, he had given her that remarkable public pledge (quoted above) to help her if she needed assistance in ending her life.

* * *

There was a serious police investigation of the circumstances of Sue's death. On January 10, 1995, a special prosecutor, Robert Johnston, Q.C., was appointed by the Attorney General's office. Johnston was charged with examining all of the police evidence and recommending either that charges be laid or that they not be laid. On June 2, 1995, his brief report was filed, with the recommendation that it be made public. In it, Johnston said there was "no substantial likelihood of conviction for any criminal offence." He allowed that Svend Robinson had been there, but it could not be proven that he assisted the suicide. Since Robinson was the only witness and he refused to disclose who the mysterious "doctor" was, nothing could be pinned on anyone.

* * *

Writing in *The Walrus* magazine in 2011, Wayne Sumner argued

> *that there is a reluctance to prosecute cases like that of Robinson and Rodriguez because of what he terms "the Morgentaler effect." He believes that, as in the Morgentaler trials, sympathetic juries would be reluctant to find the defendant guilty. Morgentaler openly defied the anti-abortion law in the* Criminal Code *at the time, openly committing acts that were clearly regarded by the law as criminal ones. But four different juries, forty-eight different jurors, all refused to find him guilty.*

So maybe Sumner is right; juries might not be willing to convict someone who, for example, put an end to Rodriguez's misery. Maybe that is why there was apparently not a concerted effort to find the mysterious doctor who was alleged to have committed the illegal act and no real pressure put on Robinson to tell who it was.

There is one trouble with this theory, though. As noted in Chapter 2 on Robert Latimer's trial, there is now in Canada a prohibition against using the sort of defence used for Morgentaler. Juries can practice nullification but no one can tell them that they can.

Jury independence and the possibility of jury nullification has been seriously obstructed in Canada since 1988. Unfortunately, today, if prosecutors go after those who humanely assist in a death, "the Morgentaler effect" is less likely to materialize.

* * *

In 1993 the Supreme Court of Canada lost the chance to do something for Canada that would have benefited thousands of Canadians over the past twenty years. But it may have been premature; we needed the intervening years and the example of what happened in other countries, to build a convincing case in court for assisted death.

The Rodriguez case did, however, have an enormous impact on public awareness of problems with Canadian law on end-of-life issues. Many thought the decision was manifestly unjust. Whereas in the Latimer case it was his punishment and his treatment at the hands of the Parole Board that were seen as being out of line, here it was the refusal of the Court to permit assistance in dying — the only assistance that could really help her — to this grievously ill woman.

In spite of this major defeat at the hands of the Supreme Court, or more accurately, perhaps, because of it, the collective Canadian view on assisted death would be forever changed.

CHAPTER 4
JOHN HOFSESS AND HIS UNDERGROUND RAILROAD

John Hofsess, who founded the Right to Die Society of Canada in 1991, is an intriguing and controversial figure. He was a friend of artists and intellectuals such as Margaret Atwood, Claude Jutra and Eike-Henner Kluge. He was disliked and mistrusted by others, including, latterly, his assistant Evelyn Martens. Since the arrest of Evelyn Martens in 2002, Hofsess has kept a very low profile, but I was able to track him down and meet him in January of 2015.

Hofsess had been a student at McMaster University in Hamilton in the mid-sixties, taking mostly English and philosophy courses. He became known as an avant-garde filmmaker and wrote and directed a number of films, including the controversial *The Columbus of Sex*, produced by Ivan Reitman and Danny Goldberg. Although, he says, the film would be considered fairly mild by today's standards, it was then thought to be very racy. Despite critical acclaim for the film, Reitman and Goldberg were arrested under Canada's decency law — the first to be so arrested. During their trial, however, they were offered $175,000 to make a feature film for MGM. The court fined them $300 and put both on probation for a year. Reitman and Goldberg went on to great fame and success in Hollywood. Reitman became particularly well known for directing and producing many major films, including *Ghostbusters*.

Hofsess had made a name for himself as a writer at McMaster and when he left there he was offered a position as film critic for *Maclean's* magazine, which he accepted and where he stayed for five years. One of his notable pieces of work was an article about the films of Stanley Kubrick, based on his own interviews with the elusive director and published in the *New York Times* on January 11, 1976.

After *Maclean's*, Hofsess worked as a freelance journalist, writing for popular publications such as *Weekend Magazine* and *Canadian Magazine*, which were at that time inserts into weekend editions of major Canadian newspapers. In the early '80s he wrote two lengthy contributions to an eight-part series on "The Future of Society" for *Homemaker Magazine*. One of the articles was about euthanasia and was based on a book by Derek Humphry called *Jean's Way: A Love Story* — an early handbook on suicide. Humphry's first wife, Jean, had committed suicide in 1975 because of her terminal cancer.

In 1990 Hofsess moved to Victoria to look after his ailing mother, who died seven months after he arrived. The loss of his mother was very stressful for Hofsess, and for some time he remembers being in a very vulnerable state of mind. He was still haunted by the death of his friend, filmmaker

Claude Jutra, who on November 5, 1986 had jumped from the Jacques Cartier Bridge in Montreal into the St. Lawrence River; his body was not found for five months. This would have been a particularly terrifying death for Jutra, Hofsess explained, because Jutra suffered from fear of heights. Jutra, at the age of fifty-three, was rapidly declining from early-onset Alzheimer's and, Hofsess said, "jumping was the one act he could manage alone." Hofsess felt guilty for not doing more to help his friend, backing away from helping him die partly because it was difficult to let go of his friend, and partly because he feared prosecution. Never again, he vowed, would he let that happen.

Hofsess gave up writing for about five years after Jutra's death. Then, while living in Victoria, he was shocked by another suicide he read about in the Victoria *Times Colonist* newspaper. Charles and Margaret Le Moir, an elderly couple living in a high-rise apartment building in the James Bay area of the city, had leapt together to their deaths out of their fourteenth-floor apartment window. Hofsess was extraordinarily moved by those few lines in the newspaper and went to the apartment to try to find out more about the couple, but the building manager could add little to what was in the newspaper. Charles had been eighty-five at the time of death, and Margaret was eighty. Charles had been a firefighter in Vancouver for thirty-five years. They both suffered from various ailments that made their lives a misery. Apparently all they could think to do about their situation was to jump together from their window. Their story quickly disappeared from the news, but Hofsess could not forget it.

There must be a better way, Hofsess thought, to end such lives. Dylan Thomas may have wanted his father to "Rage, rage, against the dying of the light," but that is not what most people want. They want to go gently into that good night. They do not want to leap from buildings or bridges, or to shoot themselves, or to starve themselves, but in many cases they just do not know what else to do. Violent endings can also cause great distress to accidental witnesses or bystanders or to those who find the bodies. And, of course, to friends and family.

Hofsess had long been seeking some way of giving purpose to his life and now maybe he had found it: helping desperate people to find better ways of dying. This, Hofsess thought, is something he could do and something he wanted to do. And no one else seemed to be really addressing the issue.

There was and is an organization based in Toronto called Dying with Dignity, but it has primarily been concerned with such matters as advance directives and lobbying government for more progressive legislation. It did not provide help to people who wanted to know how to end their lives. By this time there were also two books written by Derek Humphry — *Jean's Way* (1978) and then *Final Exit* (1991) — books that Hofsess characterized, not approvingly, as do-it-yourself manuals. He thought that what people really wanted was help in dying, not an instruction booklet. This thought guided his actions over the next several years.

Hofsess believed that most people who want to die would prefer to have more than just assistance in carrying out the act; they would like someone to do it for them — voluntary euthanasia rather than simply assisted suicide, where the dying person takes the final action. That is why he was not enamoured of Humphry's do-it-yourself books. Hofsess's view is borne out by statistics from the Netherlands, show-ing that, where a choice between the two is given, dying patients choose voluntary euthanasia over assisted suicide by a ratio of over twenty to one. In fact most would prefer to be sedated so that at the end they are really not conscious. It seems that most of us are like Woody Allen, who says that he does not fear death; he just does not want to be there when it happens.

In late 1991 Hofsess rented a large auditorium at the University of Victoria and invited three speakers: Canadian politician Svend Robinson, who had had been a vocal supporter of the right to die; Eike-Henner Kluge, the philosopher from the University of Victoria; and Derek Humphry, whose *Final Exit* had become an American bestseller. Six hundred people came to the meeting and the Right to Die Society of Canada was formed, with Hofsess as president.

Soon afterwards, in 1992, Hofsess got to know Sue Rodriguez and her desire to have assistance in dying when her ALS became too disabling. For a time, as discussed in the previous chapter, Hofsess was the main spokesperson in this case, until politician Svend Robinson and lawyer Chris Considine took over.

By 1994, Hofsess realized that the internet was providing a new and very powerful way of reaching large numbers of people. He knew that many Canadians were interested in his message of support of those who wished to end their lives, but it had been difficult to reach them. Now there was a way.

Hofsess had founded a magazine called *Last Rights*, but its reach was mostly limited to people who already knew something of the topic. Hofsess saw how the internet could vastly increase the reach of his organization. His first effort was a modest one as a "Special Interest Group" on a public site called Victoria FreeNet, based in Victoria. The site included background information on the Right to Die Society and a few articles from *Last Rights*.

Soon Hofsess had information centres set up on the National Capital FreeNet, based in Ottawa, and then on the Toronto FreeNet. The sites were increasingly sophisticated; the Toronto site had an expanded menu and links to a number of related newsgroups. In September of 1994 the Society was able to get permission to publish, electronically, the complete hearings of the Senate Special Committee on Euthanasia and Assisted Suicide — the first time the Senate had released information on the internet.

Hofsess and the Right to Die Society established an independent website called DeathNET, launched January 10, 1995. There were a thousand hits on the site within two weeks. DeathNET was a rich source of information on end-of-life issues, including not just the transcripts of the Senate Special Committee on Euthanasia and Assisted Suicide but also some of the briefs by key witnesses, such as philosophers Alister Browne and Eike-Henner Kluge. There was much other material available there as well, such as the full text of the Supreme Court of Canada decision on the Rodriguez case.

DeathNET was initially very popular and widely read, and was named by one evaluation service as the best Canadian health/medical site in both 1995 and 1996. The site was kept up for some years, but eventually went into decline as Hofsess turned his attentions to other matters.

The final report of the Senate Committee on Euthanasia and Assisted Suicide, called *Of Life and Death*, came out in 1995, and was a major disappointment to Hofsess, as well as to many others who had hoped for recommendations for significant change in Canadian law. Even the modest changes that were proposed, such as the introduction of a clause in the *Criminal Code* on "compassionate homicide," were not acted upon by Parliament.

This disappointing report came out shortly after the equally disappointing decision by the Supreme Court in the Rodriguez case, denying her the right to have assistance in dying. Hofsess concluded that there was little chance of legislative change or judicial change in the near future and he decided instead to turn his attention to more directly supporting individuals interested in finding out how they might best go about ending their lives, and to giving them assistance in carrying out the task.

In 1997 Hofsess changed the name of the organization he had founded to "Right to Die Network," rather than "Society," because it better reflected his new practical approach. A society sounds like an organization that supports and promotes certain ideas. For Hofsess, the ideas about end-of-life issues were both well established and well supported, but hopelessly blocked by politicians and judges. A network sounded more like a group of people setting about doing something about the ideas they believed in — people helping people. Hofsess hoped to establish a wide network of local chapters, all of which would try to help people wanting to die.

But what about the law? The *Criminal Code of Canada* was quite specific on the matter; Section 241(b) stating that everyone who

> . . . *aids or abets a person to commit suicide, whether suicide ensues or not, is guilty of an indictable offence and is liable to imprisonment for a term not exceeding fourteen years.*

"Abets" means encouraging a suicide in some way. But what does "aids" mean? Is it simply giving advice on how to commit suicide? That certainly could be seen as aiding. Is it providing equipment or medications for the task? Or does it require some actual helping action at the time of the death? This was not clear at the time, and that uncertainty was central to the subsequent trial of Hofsess's assistant, Evelyn Martens (see Chapter 5).

One point should be repeated here, a point that often is misunderstood in discussions of assisted death. Assisted suicide (as explained in the Introduction to this book) means the providing of some sort of help in a suicide — a self-inflicted death. If someone other than the dying person performs the final act in the death, then it is no longer, technically, an assisted suicide. It is an act of voluntary euthanasia, which means that the legal offence is not assisted suicide under Section 241(b) of the *Criminal Code*. It is murder.

What did Hofsess and Martens actually do, and were they actually guilty of committing crimes? If they simply brought a compassionate human presence to a suicide, then that probably would not be viewed as illegal (as was confirmed by the judge in Martens's trial). If they participated in some more direct way, such as by providing mild sedatives that would calm the dying person, that might well be considered as aiding the suicide. But if they, for example, provided strong sedatives to render the dying person unconscious, and then they placed a plastic bag over the unconscious person's head and turned on the helium, then that, according to the law, would be murder.

Some years later in 2004, when I attended the trial of Evelyn Martens, I learned that she had attended suicides, but I did not know, then, what had actually taken place at these sessions. Although I spoke to Martens many times during and after the trial I never asked her what, exactly, she had done. If she had committed murder it would have been very awkward to answer that question. Whatever she had done, I believed was done out of human kindness, and that was enough for me to know at the time. And I did not want to put her in the difficult position of responding. But eventually I did find out what she and Hofsess were doing when they attended suicides prior to her arrest in 2002.

* * *

In 1998, as Hofsess became more focused on directly helping people who wanted to die, he stopped publishing *Last Rights* magazine and created instead an organization called Last Rights Publications, which produced various practical, explanatory booklets on different ways of ending one's life, or "self-deliverance" as he called it. He was not opposed to suicide instead of euthanasia, for those who did not mind taking the action themselves, but he strongly felt the latter should also be available to people. The booklets on techniques for ending life were made available to members of the Right to Die Network, as were plastic "exit bags" for use in the favoured method of dying. This entailed feeding helium gas into a tube attached to the bag that fit over the dying person's head. A person using this method would just quietly lose consciousness and pass away without any sense of suffocation.

This best method, according to one of the booklets produced by Hofsess, involved the initial ingestion of the powerful sedative Rohypnol (also known as the "date rape" drug). The person taking the drug would essentially be unconscious and be incapable of proceeding with dealing with the exit bag and the administration of the helium. That would have to be done by others. This would, however, clearly be euthanasia, not suicide. And one might well have asked at the time, how did Hofsess know this was such a good technique if he had not used it to take part in at least one death? Law enforcement officials might well have asked this question if they had read Hofsess's booklets.

Rohypnol is illegal in the US and in Canada, but it widely available in other countries. It is sometimes legally used for people with sleeping problems and illegally, of course, for purposes of sexual assault. The drug is related to Valium but is seven to ten times more powerful, and acts in about fifteen minutes, making it an ideal sedative prior to voluntary euthanasia.

In 1999 Hofsess joined an international organization called NuTech — New Technologies for Self-Deliverance. NuTech was funded mainly by Derek Humphry, who had founded the American Hemlock Society in 1980 to provide information about dying and to promote physician-assisted suicide. Hofsess promoted NuTech, and organized "fieldworkers" to provide support for people who wanted to end their lives. These workers were asked to provide data to NuTech about drug doses, gas concentrations and the length of time it took people to die. These were all highly covert operations because of the legal risks involved. Still, Hofsess and NuTech were able to collect much information that was would later appear in books such as *The Peaceful Pill Handbook*. Academic researcher Russel Ogden was entrusted by NuTech to analyze the data from fieldworkers.

By 2001 the public side of the Right to Die Network was mostly taken over by Ruth von Fuchs in Toronto, who had the name changed back to the Right to Die Society.

It continues to provide information to interested people, and to argue for more permissive legislation. Last Rights Publications (though not the magazine) continued on in Victoria with Hofsess and Martens, who used revenue from sales of exit bags and booklets to continue their operation. The revenue here was not inconsiderable, Hofsess told me that one order alone from Australia was for seven thousand booklets.

On the face of it, with the information being published by Last Rights Publications, it seemed clear that somebody was taking part in assisting deaths, and probably voluntary euthanasia. Was it Hofsess and Martens?

Years later, in January of 2015 when I first met Hofsess, I asked him directly what he and Martens had actually done while attending these deaths. Enigmatically he said, "Well, we weren't just there to read them the Twenty-third Psalm." He went on to describe the euthanasia service he and Martens had operated.

Over the years various people had tried to mitigate the effects of unyielding laws on assisted death; laws that seemed, at times, to be unjust and cruel. Some juries, such as that of the Rambergs, simply refused to convict, no matter what the law said they should do. Often prosecutors would press reduced charges or judges would give lighter and sometimes suspended sentences, when they thought that assistance was given for reasons of compassion and mercy. Svend Robinson openly defied the law in attending Sue Rodriguez's death, in an act that could be seen as an act of civil disobedience. But Hofsess and Martens took matters a step further: they conducted a highly risky, secret operation providing a euthanasia service to members of the Right to Die Society (or of any other similar organization).

The actions of Hofsess and Martens were a response to what they saw as the cruelty of our laws at the time. Hofsess liked to describe what they were doing as akin to what people did to help blacks escape slavery in the southern United States. The American *Fugitive Slave Act* made it illegal to help runaway slaves, but many whites did so anyway, establishing an "underground railroad" to help blacks escape from the bondage imposed by a terrible law.

Hofsess saw the laws prohibiting assisted death as being similar to the laws supporting slavery: prohibiting assistance in dying was cruel and inhuman, prolonging the intense discomfort and suffering of terminally ill people. It was like state-sponsored torture. The law should be respected, Hofsess said to me in January of 2015, but not when it leads to such cruelty. Then, he said, we have a moral obligation to oppose it. Hofsess's way of doing this was to establish his own underground railroad and provide the sort of human kindness that was prohibited by the law.

One could not do such work and at the same time carry on a public campaign, Hofsess explained. This illegal work had to take place in secret. He recalled a story about a slave who escaped the South by being shipped to freedom in the North in a wooden box. He was so proud of himself that he boasted about it later, prompting shipping officials in the South to check large boxes more closely in the future. Hofsess simply wanted to do what he could to help as many people as possible, as quietly as he could. He had given up on the possibility, in the near future, of changing the assisted suicide law.

Hofsess told me that he and Martens were involved in nine suicides in various locations. In most of these they would act together, but one, in Nova Scotia, would have been too costly for both to attend, so in that one case Martens made one trip to visit the man and then another for the actual suicide. There was a membership fee of $35 per year, or $250 for a lifetime membership fee, to join the Right to Die Network. Members could then access information and services, including assistance in dying, at no further charge. At its peak the Society had about 1,200 members. Besides the membership fees there was some additional funding from donations.

One reason that the actions of Hofsess and Martens went undetected was that he had devised a set of guidelines to try to afford as much protection as possible against prosecution:

1.   In order to get information about assistance an individual had to have been a current member of a recognized right-to-die society for at least three months. Information was not for sale to the general public but made available to members only.

2.   In order to be a member of the Right to Die Network of Canada, an individual must sign a pledge that he or she fully supported the aims and objectives of the society.

3.   No information about assisted death was to be conveyed by insecure means.

4.   Anyone requesting aid in dying had to be visited in person on at least two occasions. During the first visit, it was considered prudent to be noncommittal about offering

assistance; the purpose of the first visit was to collect information. A decision about offering help was made by the team within seven days of the preliminary visit.

5. It was important during the first visit to find out how other family members felt about assisted death. Was there a friend, relative or neighbour who might be in opposition to the applicant's plans? It was important also to study the residence of the applicant and make note of any disadvantages in its layout and location.

6. A medical report was compiled, based on the interview and whatever medical records were available, in order to determine the health and state of mind of the applicant.

7. Assisted death was not confined to a person having a terminal illness, but there had to be compelling reasons as to why an assisted death was justified, due to the long-term risks involved.

8. Precautions were taken to prevent fingerprints, footprints or DNA from being discovered on the premises of a client: latex gloves, disposable polypropylene foot covers, and hairnets were used, and plastic cutlery or glasses that may have been used were removed.

9. If after the first visit it seemed probable that an

assisted death would ultimately be approved,
a discreet place was to be found where helium
tanks could be safely disposed of within an
hour or less from the site. Exit bags were to be
disposed of at a different location.

10.   No literature from the Right to Die Society
      of Canada was to be left on the premises of a
      client; notes, correspondence or emails that
      the client might have sent to others were to be
      destroyed by the fieldworker.

These guidelines worked well for a time, with Hofsess's
underground operation escaping the attention of law
enforcement officers. Then, according to Hofsess, an odd
thing happened to the Hofsess-Martens team. In early 2002,
and perhaps earlier, Evelyn began to operate on her own
without involving or informing Hofsess. We know that she
attended two suicides without him: one in Duncan, B.C.,
at the end of January 2002 (Monique Charest) and another
in Vancouver in mid-June 2002 (Leyanne Burchell). These
were the two incidents that were the basis of the prosecution
of Martens reviewed in Chapter 5. Martens's friend Brenda
Hurn attended the Charest suicide with Martens, but
Martens attended the Burchell suicide on her own. Hofsess
says that Martens said nothing to him about these suicides,
and that he knew nothing about them.

Why would Martens start to act on her own rather than
work with Hofsess? Maybe she did not like something about
how he carried out the operations. Maybe she thought she
could do them better or more sympathetically, or something. Maybe she just preferred the company of her friend

Brenda Hurn. Hofsess did not know why this happened. He thought that the two women, and especially Hurn, did not like him very much. He once asked Hurn why Martens no longer told him about what she was doing, but Hurn only said, "Did you ever think that maybe she was trying to protect you?" But this did not sound right to him, and in fact, because she was careless about protocols, her actions did not protect him: they caused him to have to close down the entire operation.

I got to know Evelyn Martens at her trial in 2004, but she was reluctant to talk about Hofsess. She died in 2011, years before I was able to talk to Hofsess in early 2015, so I was able to get only his perspective on the relationship between the two of them. I did track down Brenda Hurn, who was living in a care facility in Victoria, but she claimed to remember very little from that time. I was not sure whether this was a standard defensive response, carrying over from when she herself might be prosecuted (it was highly unlikely at this point), or whether she really could not remember. I think the latter, as she was probably over ninety by this time.

The riskiness of what Hofsess and Martens, and later Martens and Hurn, were doing became evident on June 26, 2002, when Martens was arrested as she drove off the ferry in Sidney, British Columbia. She was trying to return to her home in Langford, near Victoria on Vancouver Island. She had been in Vancouver to attend the suicide of the morbidly ill Leyanne Burchell. Martens was charged with assisting the suicides of Burchell and of Duncan resident Monique Charest, whose suicide Martens had attended some months earlier.

This was the start of two and half years of legal proceedings for Martens, involving brief imprisonment, being shackled while being moved about, extensive interrogations of her and of her relatives and friends and frequent police harassment, and ending with her lengthy trial in Duncan, B.C., in the fall of 2004.

Following the arrest of Evelyn Martens, Hofsess abandoned NuTech and his efforts to provide support and information to those seeking to end their lives. In 2004 Last Rights Publications was permanently closed down. The heat was now on with the prosecution in progress and Hofsess, fearing arrest himself, dropped out of sight. His underground railroad was no more.

When Martens was arrested, Hofsses left his flat on Dallas Road in Victoria, went to stay with friends in the United States for a time, and then lived with other friends in Victoria. Eventually he moved into assisted housing in Victoria, where he still lived at the time of this writing. He had been lying low, because of the Martens prosecution, but as far as he could tell the police never even tried to contact him — no messages at his old address, nothing. Apparently the police did not know, or for some reason did not care, or somehow could not accommodate the fact that the engineer of the underground railroad was Hofsess.

I asked Hofsess how he had felt about the loss of the underground operation he had successfully operated for several years. His main regret was that after 2004 and the Martens trial, which forced him to shut down the service he had been offering, there was no longer any way that desperate people could get assistance in dying — at least not the humane sort of assistance Hofsess and his operation had provided.

"Would you have continued if Martens had not been arrested?" I asked.

He thought for a moment, and said quietly, "Helping those people was the best thing I ever did in my life."

"But if such things are allowed, is there not a possibility of abuse?"

"Of course," he answered. "That is why I instituted the protocols. But I am not advocating what I did as the answer — it was the only humane alternative at the time. It would be much better if we had a progressive law so that dying, when necessary and wanted, could take place openly and with safeguards. The underground railroad, though illegal at the time in the United States, was the only way to help desperate slaves trying to escape the oppression of unconscionable laws. But that was not a permanent solution. The real solution was emancipation and instatement of personal freedom. And that is also the case with assisted death."

"Do you think that your actions might have brought us closer to a better law?" I asked.

"I hope so," he said.

What was the significance of Hofsess's underground railroad? What impact did it have on the movement to decriminalize assisted suicide? It is hard to say. His impact was great for those who availed themselves of his euthanasia service, but apparently they were relatively few. Other than for those people, Hofsess's operations were kept intentionally secret. Rather than try to seek legal change he went underground to help individuals, and in doing so could not be of much help to the movement for more progressive legislation. Ironically, the greatest public impact of Hosess's underground railroad came as a result of the arrest and prosecution of his colleague Evelyn Martens, something that apparently occurred because of her carelessness in regard to the protocols he had established. Her arrest meant that the underground operation would collapse and the euthanasia service would disappear, but it did bring enormous publicity to and sympathy for the right-to-die movement.

Some may think that Hofsess's euthanasia service should be kept hidden, but we should not try to hide the past — to launder history — even if it harms a particular cause we may be interested in. We must try to present history as accurately as possible so that those who come later will know what really happened in our times, whatever that may be.

My second thought is that I think that the reaction to what Hofsess and Martens did will not be entirely unfavourable. He was a man who was appalled by the violent ways some desperate people chose to end their lives. No one, he thought, should have to die in that way. I believe that he was truly moved by the plight of such people, and he found a way to do something about it. So far as I can tell this came from a strong humanitarian impulse: he risked his own freedom to help those in need. He broke the law not for self-serving purposes but because the law came into conflict with his conscience. My hope is that he will be seen not as a figure who discredited the right-to-die movement but as one who put his own life on the line in support of his belief in the movement, and as such should be accorded much respect and esteem.

One more thing should be said about Hofsess and his accomplishments. He started the Canadian Right to Die Society and was therefore responsible for the many ways this organization affected the development of the movement in Canada. The organization and its offshoots provided information about dying to many thousands of people over the years and was behind two of the most famous Canadian legal cases on the matter — those of

Sue Rodriguez and Evelyn Martens. It is doubtful that the public support that resulted in striking down the law on assisted suicide would have come about without Hofsess's Right to Die Society.

CHAPTER 5
THE TRIAL OF EVELYN MARTENS — 2004

September 20, 2004, in the Supreme Court of British Columbia, City of Duncan:

Evelyn Marie Martens of Langford, British Columbia, stands charged:

Count 1

That she, the said Evelyn Marie Martens, on or about the 7th day of January, 2002, at the city of Duncan, in the Province of British Columbia, did unlawfully aid and/or abet the suicide of Monique Charest contrary to Section 241(b) of the *Criminal Code*.

Count 2

That she, the said Evelyn Marie Martens, on or about the 26th day of June, 2002, at the city of Vancouver, in the Province of British Columbia, did unlawfully aid and/or abet the suicide of Leyanne Burchell contrary to Section 241(b) of the *Criminal Code*.

* * *

The underground movement organized by John Hofsess was suddenly struck by the brutal reality of flouting the law on June 26, 2002. His associate was arrested and charged with assisted suicide. Evelyn Martens, a seventy-four-year-old grandmother, was facing the prospect of as much as twenty-eight years in prison. It could have been worse. Had the authorities known what probably did take place at these deaths, the charge could have been murder. Hofsess's underground railroad shut down forever and Hofsess himself disappeared. His life's work was over.

The trial, which I attended in full, began on the cool morning of September 20, 2004 in the small courthouse in Duncan, British Columbia. Outside, before the proceedings began, a milling crowd of photographers, reporters, television cameramen and other observers waited. Suddenly everyone turned toward a small, elderly, almost frail, figure approaching from the courthouse parking lot. Evelyn Martens had arrived. Without stopping or speaking to the reporters, she went directly into the courthouse.

The trial followed a two-year police investigation during which Martens had been the target of an elaborate undercover operation, then arrested and jailed, and had to struggle even to get bail. Police repeatedly searched her home, confiscating anything they found of relevance to their investigation. In the runup to the trial Martens was subjected to abusive accusations by the Euthanasia Prevention Coalition (EPC); at one point their newsletter carried the headline "Death Zealot Kills Two." Now, after lengthy pretrial sessions, Martens's trial was about to begin. She could end up going to prison for the rest of her life.

This was not the first prosecution in Canada for assisted suicide. In 1949 the Inuit Eerkiyoot and his cousin Ishakak were found guilty of the assisted suicide of his mother (see Chapter 1), but, largely because what they did was related to traditional Inuit customs, Eerkiyoot was given a light sentence and Ishakak a suspended one. In 1963 there was another similar prosecution of Inuits Amah, Avinga and Nangmalik, all of whom were also given suspended sentences.

In 1986 Lois Wilson pleaded guilty to assisting the suicide of her boyfriend and was given a six-month sentence (see Chapter 1). In 1995 Mary Jane Fogarty was convicted in Nova Scotia for assisting the suicide of her friend Brenda Barnes and was given a suspended sentence, plus three hundred hours of community service work. In 1997 Maurice Genereux was given two years less a day for assisting the suicide of an HIV patient. He became the first doctor to be convicted of assisted suicide.

There had been a number of other Canadian cases involving some form of assisted death, which mostly led to light or suspended sentences (see Chapter 1 and Appendix 1). Also, there had been the Rodriguez case (see Chapter 3), where a crime had definitely been committed but a special prosecutor declined to pursue the matter on the grounds that evidence sufficient for a conviction was unlikely.

Now, in 2004, a very determined prosecution of Evelyn Martens was underway. The authorities meant business with this one, partly because Martens was not just helping a friend or relative in distress but had been attending the suicides of people she did not know very well. She had been a key part of the underground team, providing an illegal euthanasia service, organized by John Hofsess and the Right to Die Network of Canada. And she had been caught. Or had she?

The police had conducted a lengthy and expensive investigation, and appeared to be focused, this time, on seeing that the defendant was suitably punished for her alleged crimes. Sympathy had been shown to those such as Eerkiyoot, Lois Wilson and Mary Jane Fogarty because they had been helping a friend or a relative escape their pain. But Martens seemed to be participating in a larger, organized scheme. The police talked darkly of some sort of international death ring.

Martens had, in fact, been actively participating in the deaths of members of the Right to Die Network. So had Hofsess. According to Hofsess, they had worked together on several assisted deaths and Martens had attended at least two more without him — the ones she was being prosecuted for. It was not exactly an international crime ring, although Martens and Hofsess had attended at least one suicide in the United States. But it was, Hofsess told me, a criminal operation. He said that in the cases of the deaths they attended together, both he and Martens had been guilty of committing voluntary euthanasia, which if known at the time would have resulted in a murder charge, not just assisted suicide.

I never did know if the two deaths being investigated in the Martens trial had also been cases of voluntary euthanasia, or assisted suicide, or neither, as her lawyers claimed in court.

* * *

Who was this woman? Was she some sort of merchant of
death, or as the EPC had claimed, a "death zealot"?

She had lived most of her life in Alberta, where she was
married three times and had six children. From early photos
of her I could see that she had been a very beautiful young
woman. She devoted her early life to raising the children
and then worked for the Alberta Liquor Control Board for
sixteen years. In 1989 she retired and moved to Langford,
near Victoria.

A year before she moved to British Columbia Evelyn's
beloved brother Cornelius, who lived in Ottawa, became
terminally ill from bone cancer. Evelyn and her sisters Kay
and Gwen travelled to be with Cornelius in his final days in
the hospital, and they took turns spending every night with
him as he lay suffering through a prolonged and agonizing
death. Other family members also came to visit and joined
in the vigil. As Cornelius worsened and his pain became
nearly unbearable – too much even for the strong doses
of morphine he was given — Evelyn and her sisters went
to the doctor to ask him to do something more to relieve
Cornelius's suffering.

The doctor said anything more would kill him, and if he
did that, he said, "it will be on your shoulders." It struck
Evelyn as an odd thing to say — for the doctor to imply that
there would something wrong about hastening Cornelius's
death. Earlier, when he could still write, Cornelius had written a note saying, "If there is a God, please take me now. I
can't stand the pain."

The pain became so bad that Evelyn and the others
insisted that the dose of morphine be increased. Then, to

everyone's great relief, Cornelius died shortly thereafter.

Evelyn was deeply affected by this experience. Why, she wondered, should people have to suffer in such a way, when there was no possibility of recovery, no hope for any sort of bearable life? The Catholic Church, to which she had once belonged, claimed that suffering just had to be tolerated, but to Evelyn it was like the priests denying women birth control: none of them had ever carried a child or been forced to live in poverty with too many children. None of them had ever been in the sort of agony Cornelius had been in. That unnecessary suffering weighed heavily on Evelyn. To her, it was just not right.

In 1989 Evelyn happened to meet John Hofsess, who shortly afterwards founded the Right to Die Society of Canada. Evelyn joined in 1990. "It was because of my brother's death," she told me. "I didn't want to die that way, and I didn't want others to have to do so either. I always have felt a lot of compassion for others; it sometimes gets me into trouble. I feel their pain — it's just who I am."

Martens began to volunteer for Hofsess's organization, initially stuffing envelopes and helping with mail-outs. She began to take on more and more of a workload and soon became the main contact person for the organization.

As Martens became immersed in the work of the organization she realized how very many people wanted information about how they might escape an undignified, prolonged and painful death. Word of the organization spread and Martens took enquiries from many people from many different countries. One woman from Ireland, Rosemary Toole-Gilhooly, phoned at least twenty times. Unknown to Hofsess, Martens broke protocol when she exchanged numerous emails with Toole-Gilhooly. To Hofsess, emails were far too insecure. These emails did in fact become a major reason for the prosecution of Martens, when the Irish police force found them when investigating the death of Toole-Gilhooly. The information was given to the RCMP, who then began the investigation of Martens. Hofsess had been right about his protocols.

Martens was also careless when she left a business card with Monique Charest, whose death was attended by Martens. When the police found the card they made a connection with the information they had received from Ireland.

Martens was going to go to Ireland to help with the death of Toole-Gilhooly, if her travel costs could be reimbursed by the Irish woman, but instead it was decided that American assisted-suicide activist George Exoo would go instead. Toole-Gilhooly was a wealthy woman and she left a sizable bequest for both Martens and Exoo, but this was denied on appeal by the Irish courts, on the grounds that one should not profit from an illegal activity. It should be pointed out that money did not ever seem to be the driving force for Hofsess and Martens; otherwise they could have charged much more for their services.

* * *

In the fourteen years Martens worked for the Right to Die Society, she took a great many calls from people who wanted information on how to end their lives, or at least to be in a position to do so should their conditions worsen. There is no evidence or reason to believe that she ever tried to encourage anyone to end his or her life.

Hofsess and Martens both knew that they could get into trouble with the law, although Hofsess was clearly the more cautious of the two, with his protocols. Both felt very strongly that people had a right to know how they could end their lives in a dignified way, and they had a right to have help with this if they wanted it. How could it be wrong to give people the peace of mind of knowing that there was a way of avoiding a terrible death?

Hofsess and Martens knew that helping people die, under current Canadian law, was illegal, but they were also very sure it was not wrong. They knew of many instances where people in desperation had taken drastic steps such as shooting themselves, leaving the grisly remains for family members to find. *That* was wrong. They knew of others, like Cornelius, who desperately wanted to escape to a peaceful death but was forced to linger on in agony. *That* was wrong.

Moreover, if these acts of mercy were such heinous crimes, and not just arbitrary rules passed by politicians, then why were other countries passing laws that allowed both assisted suicide and voluntary euthanasia? Both the Netherlands and Belgium did so in 2002. Hofsess and Martens were not breaking some sacred universal law; they were breaking a law that was being recognized as unnecessary and cruel by other countries.

Was Evelyn Martens a death zealot who ought to spend the rest of her own life in prison, as the Euthanasia Prevention Coalition claimed? Or was she a kind-hearted person who found she was able to provide comfort to desperate people who could find it nowhere else? I came to believe it was the latter, but if it could be proven she was guilty of assisting death it would not matter much what she was — she would be going to prison.

Although Martens was in serious trouble, she had a couple of things going for her. Polls consistently showed that majority of Canadians supported her. Maybe we would see jury nullification. Furthermore, the prosecution was going to have difficulty in proving what exactly had taken place at these deaths. There was clear evidence that Martens had attended the two suicides in question — this was never in any real dispute. Moreover it was pretty obvious that she had gone to see the two women *because* of their planned suicides, so she had undoubtedly offered advice on how and what to do. But would that be enough? The trial judge, Justice Barry Davies clarified this by stating that attendance and advice were not enough. Something more concrete had to happen before reaching the threshold for aiding. Something more probably did happen, as we now know from John Hofsess, but the prosecution would have difficulty proving it.

Aiding could also mean helping if something went wrong, which was something Martens admitted (to an undercover agent) was a reason she attended these suicides. One of the fears people have in wanting to commit suicide is that they might for some reason not fully complete the task, and be left alive with serious brain damage, in an even worse condition than that which made them want to die in the first place, and without the physical ability to complete the job at another time. One of the women who died — Monique Charest — had suffered from visions of becoming trapped in a non-functioning body, unable to do anything to end her miserable plight.

However, even with Martens admitting she had been willing to intervene if needed, it is difficult to see how she could be convicted for assisting because she was prepared to intervene, if she had not actually done so. And there was no evidence to show that she had.

Abetting suicide — actively encouraging suicide or, in

some serious way, inciting a person to take his or her own life
— was never an issue in the trial. Any evidence on possible
abetting was all in Martens's favour: Brenda Hurn, Martens's
friend who attended the Charest suicide with her, and who
was subpoenaed to testify, indicated that after a long talk
with Ms. Charest, Brenda and Evelyn had suggested that she
wait a few more months to be sure this was what she wanted,
and that then they would be happy to come back and see her
again, and be with her if by then she was still sure this was
what she wanted to do. And this was supported by what was
found in the undercover operation, discussed below.

Martens's defence would be that she had gone only to give
advice, comfort and emotional support to the two women in
their last moments of life, but that she had taken no action
to physically assist in the process. The prosecution's job
was to prove, beyond a reasonable doubt, that Martens did
participate in these deaths more than just by attending or
giving advice. This was a difficult task, because there had
been no detailed revelations about what actually took place
at these events

* * *

There were many dramatic moments in the trial that saw
thirty-eight witnesses provided by the prosecution and none
by the defence. Sometimes, particularly near the end of the
trial, the observer seats were almost full, with perhaps fifty
or so people. Martens's son, Les Poelzer, quit his job in
Alberta so he could attend the complete trial. But people
hostile to Martens were always there too. During a few
days near the end of the trial a severely disabled person was
wheeled into the courtroom, apparently as an unofficial

exhibit. This was meant to convey the idea that if someone like Martens was allowed to facilitate deaths then we would end up forcing euthanasia on handicapped people, like the one in the wheelchair.

All of us there, whatever our views on the matter, probably came to one common opinion: this would be a landmark trial in regard to the law on assisted suicide.

Besides that, though, there was the real question of what would happen to this grandmother who had been under investigation for two years by the formidable combined forces of the RCMP and the Crown Prosecutor's office. They had spent a lot of money investigating and prosecuting this case.

Martens seemed to remain unruffled during the proceedings — standing straight when the jury and judge entered the Court, and then sitting calmly beside her lawyers, Peter Firestone and Catherine Tyhurst of Victoria. While her supporters often seemed nervous and uneasy, Martens showed little sign of concern. She felt strongly she had done nothing wrong and that she had helped people in severe distress who could find help nowhere else. She was prepared to accept whatever they wanted to do to her now.

The Undercover Operation

A supposedly key piece of evidence against Martens was a recording of her conversation with an RCMP undercover agent posing as the goddaughter of Monique Charest. The ruse was that the goddaughter was upset by Charest's death and wanted to talk to someone who knew what had happened. Martens fell for it and kindly agreed to meet the woman in Vancouver. The resulting recording seemed to be regarded by the prosecution as proof of guilt.

However, the recording, which was played in full for the jury, seemed more helpful to the defence than to the prosecution. I wondered why they even used it. For one thing it showed Martens as a very compassionate woman who, albeit naively, went out of her way to meet the youngish woman and comfort her about the loss of her supposed godmother. Martens went to some trouble to do this, something she did not need to do.

The recording also provided evidence that Martens had tried to dissuade Monique Charest from her suicide. In these open and unguarded comments, Martens appeared to be a warm, kindly woman motivated only by the desire to help people in distress, as she was also trying to do by meeting to talk with the upset goddaughter.

It was annoyingly difficult to get a transcript of the undercover operation, which I needed because it was impossible to hear or record it all as it was playing in the courtroom. It took me about a month, with frequent requests made to the prosecutor's office and the records department. Finally, after being told a number of times that it was not possible to get the transcript, I said that could not be true. The comments were part of the public record and it was absurd to say that my only access to this public information was to listen to a somewhat inaudible recording in the courtroom. Persistence finally prevailed, and the courthouse office released the transcript to me.

When I talked about this operation with Hofsess, he pointed out that this had happened after Martens had gone her own way in attending suicides. He said he would have been immediately suspicious if he had heard about some goddaughter wanting to talk about one of the suicides. Martens's immediate response was to help the person in distress. Hofsess would have smelled a rat.

THE DEATH OF MONIQUE CHAREST

Realizing that they would need to provide evidence that Martens did more than simply be present at Monique Charest's suicide, the Crown tried to argue that Martens had provided Charest with equipment and sedatives used in the death. Their argument was based on autopsy evidence that Charest had phenobarbital in her blood and no prescriptions for that particular drug had been given to her by her doctor, and no phenobarbital vials were found in her apartment after her death. The suggestion was that Martens must have supplied the drug and then removed the evidence. But there were other possible sources of the drug, and other things that might have happened to any empty vials, so it was impossible to prove that Martens had been involved in this.

Somewhat more problematic for Martens' defence was the matter of the equipment, particularly the "exit bag" that had been used by Charest. It was acknowledged by the defence that Martens and Brenda Hurn, Martens's friend who also attended this death, had taken a satchel to the apartment (a witness had confirmed this), but Hurn testified that the satchel had been empty and was for the purpose of removing the equipment that Charest already had. The Crown, on the other hand, suggested that the satchel contained the equipment and was brought by the two women for the sole purpose of aiding a suicide and that they had then removed it to hide evidence of their involvement.

But the defence had plausible rebuttals of this. The prosecution has to prove its allegations; the defence just needs to provide reasonable alternative explanations. The defence lawyers said that Charest had obtained the exit bag previously, which was not an illegal thing to do for buyer or seller, and she had herself had obtained the helium tank, which would have been readily available from toy stores for filling balloons. There were at least two places where tanks might have been purchased within blocks of where Charest lived.

This argument was supported by the fact that literature on assisted dying recommends exactly this sort of protocol: getting the drugs and equipment separately so that anyone attending would be less likely to be seen as assisting.

Nor did removal of the equipment imply guilt. There was evidence that Charest had, in fact, requested that Martens remove the equipment after she died because, oddly, she didn't want the Church to know that she had ended her own life. She had been a nun earlier in life and still carried with her, to some extent, the strictures of the Church.

There was another good reason, in addition to Charest's request, for Martens to remove the equipment. Martens, though less attentive to protocol details than Hofsess would have been, was not unaware of the possibility of prosecution. Leaving evidence of suicide might lead police to investigate possible assistance. So apart from the reason Charest had for concealing the suicide, Martens herself had a good reason for what she did in removing the equipment, whether or not she had brought the equipment in the first place.

The exit bag, however, was a bit more problematic for the defence. Brenda Hurn admitted that Charest used a bag with a tube attached, and a Velcro collar to go around the neck, a bag of the kind that had been sold by Martens and the right-to-die organization for which she volunteered. Unlike the helium tanks, these were not available in toy stores. When police searched Martens's house they found several such bags. Did it not seem likely that she was supplying these to people, thus aiding suicides?

And in fact Martens had been doing this, something she could scarcely conceal, since the evidence for this was found in her house. However, giving or selling such bags in itself is not illegal, any more than selling a gun to someone who subsequently uses it for suicide makes the act of selling it illegal. One cannot make the assumption that the gun, or the bag, is going to be used for the purpose of suicide. The bag, for example, might be wanted for purposes of some sort of demonstration — even the opponents of assisted suicide might want one for that purpose.

The Crown had to prove that Martens had brought the bag on the specific day of the suicide, for that specific purpose, and then they might have been able to make a case for assisted suicide. They could not do this.

Although Martens might well have brought an exit bag for Charest, there was no way to prove that she had. Charest might have obtained the bags elsewhere, as the literature that she had had in her possession had recommended. Or she might even have obtained them from Martens at an earlier date, which would not likely have been grounds for conviction. But whatever the case, it could not be proven.

* * *

To the annoyance of Justice Davies, the Crown made much of Charest's state of health. They were determined to prove that Charest was not really very ill. Davies could not see the relevance of this point to the charge of aiding suicide. Martens's guilt or innocence, according to law, did not depend on whether or not either of these suicides were carried out by deathly ill women, but on whether or not Martens had aided them. The two women could have been in the best of health and the legal question would be the same: did Martens aid the suicide of one or both of them?

Juries, however, consist of ordinary people who sometimes make decisions for emotional reasons. The arguments about Charest's health — that it had not been too bad — could influence how the jury reacted to the case. If Charest had been in good health then the jury may well have been more inclined to think Martens's actions in assisting, whatever exactly they were, unjustified. The prior health of the deceased ought not to have had any influence whatsoever on the verdict, but a guilty judgment was more likely if jurors felt that Charest should not have died. It was unlikely any juror would have felt that about Leyanne Burchell, given the grim testimony about her illness (see below). Charest, though, could likely have gone on living for some time.

There may have been another reason for why the Crown made such an effort to sway the jury's feeling by portraying Charest as a relatively healthy woman. They may have been concerned about the possibility of jury nullification — finding Martens not guilty even if she was technically guilty. This right of a jury comes into play when jury members are sympathetic with the accused, and when they feel that a guilty verdict, though legally correct, would be unjust. The Crown may well have reasoned that, even if a successful case could be made against Martens, the jury, out of concern about the injustice of a guilty verdict, might find Martens not guilty. Creating the impression that Charest should not have died, then, and that Martens contributed to this premature death, could undermine the prospect of nullification.

At great length the Crown described Charest as a woman with some health problems, none of which were terribly serious. The Crown had called in Charest's doctor, who testified that Charest had not been terminally ill and that he did not believe she really had a serious disease — acute intermittent porphyria — that she thought she had.

In cross-examination Catherine Tyhurst pointed out that Charest's doctor had signed a "Do Not Resuscitate" form for her. These are standard forms used by terminally ill people who do not want efforts made to bring them back to life, should they lose consciousness and begin to die. The forms specify that they are to be used *only* for patients who are terminally ill or who are "near the end of their natural life." Tyhurst pointed out that signing the document must have indicated to Charest that, in her doctor's judgment, she was terminally ill (since Charest was only sixty and not near the end of her "natural life"). The document required his signature three times, and concludes with a statement that the statement reflects his medical opinion.

The doctor's explanation of this discrepancy was a feeble one — that Charest really was not terminally ill, but there were only a limited number of forms and sometimes they did not exactly fit the circumstance.

"You could have written something on the form to fix it, couldn't you?" Tyhurst asked. "But you didn't, did you?"

"No, I didn't," he replied.

Tyhurst then took a close look at the terminal disease Charest believed she had — acute intermittent porphyria. In his testimony the doctor had said that she did not have the disease. But he admitted referring her to a clinic in Winnipeg that was one of the few that specialized in treating this disease. The doctor had testified that a test Charest had taken for the disease was negative, but under cross-examination admitted that the test had been inconclusive.

It became clear that Charest, and Martens, had good

reason to believe that she was terminally ill. The Crown's attempt to use Monique's health to turn the jury against Martens fell completely flat after Catherine Tyhurst's cross-examination of Charest's doctor.

THE DEATH OF LEYANNE BURCHELL

There was no doubt regarding the terminal condition of Leyanne Burchell when she, with Martens present, died. Her doctor had seen her on June 19, 2002, shortly before her death on June 26, and he described her as being close to the end of her life. He said that her stomach cancer had spread to her bowel and was progressing toward a total obstruction that would prevent her from eating. The blockage was too high up to allow the use of a bag to collect food that she swallowed. If she tried to eat it would just cause her to vomit. When complete blockage occurred she would not even be able to swallow her own saliva. There was nothing that could be done to prevent her death. The doctor thought she might live another thirty days.

Burchell's abdominal pain was so severe, her sister Denise Huguet testified, that morphine no longer could control it. Burchell developed her own way of coping with the pain, by using a scalding hot water bottle on her abdomen. This added a new pain that distracted her from the unrelenting internal agony of her cancer, but the bottle was so hot it actually burned her skin and turned it black. If you were around her when she did this you could smell the burnt flesh. Huguet said that her sister was terrified about the possibility of internal gases being trapped by the blockage. Doctors had told her this might cause her to explode from inside.

But even Burchell's desperate condition did not persuade some that assisting her death was warranted. Euthanasia

Prevention Coalition spokesperson Beverly Welsh, a retired palliative care nurse, talked to the press about how tragic it was for family when someone took his or her own life. Had Welsh actually talked to Burchell's family she might have reconsidered this view. On a couple of occasions I did talk to Burchell's mother, who had quietly attended a few days of the trial. She told me that she and other family members were deeply grateful for what Evelyn Martens had done.

The forensic pathologist who conducted an autopsy on Burchell's body stated that he believed the cause of death to be a drug overdose. He believed that Burchell had taken a lethal dose of a mixture of several different drugs. There was no direct evidence that she had used helium or an exit bag, though the Crown tried hard, at first, to make a case that she had, largely because two empty helium tanks and a used exit bag were found in Martens's van when she was arrested later on the evening of Burchell's death. The police apparently thought they had caught her red-handed with the necessary evidence for prosecution. But then in came the pathologist's report and his assessment that the cause of death was a drug overdose, not helium. Helium still could have been used, of course, but any sign of it would have dissipated by the time the body was examined

At this point the Crown's case became muddled. They had initially argued that the evidence of the tanks and exit bags in the van proved that Martens was guilty. Then, after the pathologist's report about the drug overdose, they tried to argue that Martens had supplied the drugs — with no real evidence to support this claim. None of this was at all convincing.

John Hofsess told me that if the police had read his booklets on "The Art and Science of Suicide," which he believes they had in their possession, they would have better understood that both drugs and helium were normally used in the suicides he and Evelyn were involved in. It was not one or the other. A more informed prosecution team might have made the case that the drugs went along with the helium. The pathologist should have been aware of this as well, and not taken such a categorical position on the cause of death.

THE VERDICT

At the conclusion of the presentation of the case against Martens, and after closing statements by both sides, Justice Davies gave his instructions to the jury. Davies told the jury how to proceed and how to evaluate evidence. He also gave a lengthy summary of the cases for both sides. The jury had not been allowed to discuss the evidence until they were sent out for deliberations, after the judge's instructions, so it was likely that there were things they had to sort through.

Given Justice Davies' definition of aiding — that it had to be more than offering comfort and advice — I thought that even if Martens had broken the law (which I thought was likely, after hearing John Hofsess's comments eleven years later) the case against her was weak. The prosecution had not proven that she had done anything that would, by the judge's definition, constitute aiding. Still, I was not at all sure what was going to happen. On the second day of jury deliberations, November 4, 2004, Beverly Welsh of the Euthanasia Prevention Coalition continued to express her confidence, to any who would listen, that Martens would be found guilty. I knew one of us must be wrong, but I could not be sure which of us it was.

Clearly, Martens's friends and relatives were uneasy. All that was needed for a hung jury was one stubborn opponent of assisted suicide, and that would be no victory for Martens. A new trial might be then held, and she would have to go through the trauma and expense all over again. Worse though, for Martens, would be if she were found guilty, and that was still a real possibility. None of us knew what would happen.

Around noon on that second day the jury came back into the courtroom to ask two questions:

> *Can members of the jury base their decision on one piece of evidence, namely the taped conversation between Ms. Martens and the undercover agent? Is this enough to reach a verdict without any further evidence to support it?*

This was the first clue anyone had as to what was going on with the jury, but what did it tell us? It was a puzzle. The questions suggested that at least one juror was concerned about something in the undercover tapes, but what was it? Was there something that was viewed as clearly incriminating? Or was the tape seen, instead, exculpatory, and one or more jurors thought that this alone was enough to find her innocent? And did the questions reflect a single idiosyncratic position, or something that concerned many, or most, or all of the jurors?

My first thought was that at least one juror felt there was something inescapably incriminating on the tape. During the next break I asked others in attendance what they thought it meant. Les Poelzer, Evelyn's son, was particularly worried about one statement his mother had made in the undercover interview, speaking of Charest's death:

> *She just didn't want to be alone. She didn't want to wake up and still be here. And that's where I came in.*

Some jurors might have taken this as an admission of guilt, because it seemed to suggest that Martens was at least willing to take some sort of action. The phrase "And that's where I came in" particularly worried Poelzer. This phrase was in fact subsequently cited in a Canadian Broadcasting Corporation (CBC) documentary as proof of guilt, a view that I think was incorrect.

Perhaps in saying "And that's where I came in" Martens was admitting she intervened in the suicide in a manner that would be considered to be "assisting suicide" according to the judge's interpretation of the law. This might have been a plausible argument except that it conveniently ignores what Martens said immediately afterwards, something that was not mentioned by the CBC. The conversation proceeded in this way:

> *AGENT. Okay and she took enough that you*
> *didn't . . .*
> *MARTENS. . . . Yeah . . .*
> *AGENT. . . . have to . . .*
> *MARTENS. . . . nothing . . .*
> *AGENT. . . . do anything extra or? Oh dear.*

"Oh dear," indeed — there goes the case. Exactly contrary to the CBC's claim, this exchange is exculpatory, not proof of guilt. Martens explicitly said that she did nothing to assist in the process, in unguarded comments to a supposed confidant, not knowing that the police were listening in. This was, as we now know, not the whole story, but as evidence of guilt this excerpt from the undercover operation provided nothing of value to the prosecution.

Another statement from the recording of the undercover

operation, that may have generated the jury question, occurred when Martens was again speaking of Charest:

> *But she was so happy we were helping her with it [the suicide] . . . I've helped other people and I've never had anyone that wasn't very, very happy to go.*

This was a direct admission of "helping," which someone might take as admission of guilt. After all, isn't helping the same as aiding? But helping is too vague a term to meet the standard for aiding, as defined by Justice Davies. However, one or more of the jurors might have taken that sentence, in isolation, as an admission of guilt.

Another possibility was that the opposite had happened — that one or more jurors found the tape so compelling that they could not find this woman guilty, regardless of whatever else the prosecution presented.

After lunch the Court reconvened, without the jury, to discuss the questions. The prosecution and the defence each made presentations about how to respond to the questions. Eventually Justice Davies called the jury back in, explained the difficulties they were having about the precise meaning of the questions. He reread some of the instructions from the previous day, when he had explained the role of the jury, and then he told them that if they based a guilty verdict on one piece of evidence they could do so, as long as they were satisfied that the single piece of evidence was sufficient to prove guilt or innocence; there was no legal requirement for supporting evidence.

It had been an odd day, with the strange questions from the jury, questions that still left us unsure about what they were thinking. What would happen next? Were these the last few hours of Martens's freedom? With the weeks of testimony, and long hours of waiting, and the scrums with media, and the talks in the corridor during breaks in proceedings, it was difficult to think that it all could suddenly end, at any moment. It felt instead that was just going to drift on indefinitely.

All of us there — reporters like me, friends and relatives of Evelyn Martens, cameramen, Beverly Welsh and others from the Euthanasia Prevention Coalition — all waited together. I could not predict what was going to happen, nor could most people there. Beverly Welsh, however, continued to radiate confidence.

At about 5:00 p.m., when most of us were thinking of going home, there was a bit of activity in the corridor — something was happening. I caught Catherine Tyhurst going into the judge's chambers and she said all of the lawyers had been called in. She did not know what was going on.

Then, maybe twenty minutes later, the Court reconvened. I was expecting that the lawyers would be responding to some issue the judge had brought up in chambers — maybe another question from the jury. But then the jury filed in. Suddenly it dawned on me that this was it. It was happening now. The jury had decided.

Everyone in the courtroom stood up as the judge entered.

Martens too rose and stood calmly. I wondered, if the verdict was guilty, if she would be taken away in shackles, as she had been when first arrested.

The end came with shocking suddenness. The clerk read out the first of the two charges — the Charest charge, the more problematic one. I glanced at Martens. What she was about to hear, whatever it was, would profoundly affect the rest of her life. She waited calmly. I glanced at her son Les

Poelzer. He had his hands up to his mouth.

The jury foreman said, "We find the defendant not guilty."

And we all knew at that moment, even before the foreman read the second verdict, that Martens was free.

* * *

The Martens trial and the Rodriguez ruling were, at the time they happened, distressing revelations of the inadequacy of Canadian law in regard to end-of-life matters. There was a human need out there that was not being served, especially among the aged and infirm. People fear death, but they also fear how they will die — most want a gentle, painless death. Martens and Hofsess, when they worked together, apparently helped people have such a death, by committing illegal acts of euthanasia. Martens probably did the same when working on her own or with Brenda Hurn.

No one thinks that the underground operation being run by these two was the way assistance in dying should be provided to those who want it — not Hofsess, not Martens, when they were alive. Both of them believed it would be much better to have a public process with safeguards. They only did what they did because there was no legal process to help these desperate people.

At the time of the Martens trial in 2004 many people had a feeling that maybe at last there would be some positive steps taken toward improving end-of-life legislation. There was feeling of momentum in the air. Besides the Martens trial there was the recent memory of the ordeal of Sue Rodriguez and the ongoing trauma of Robert

Latimer (see Chapter 2). Federal Justice Minister Irwin Cotler was quoted as saying that maybe it was time to look at the matter again. Further generating public interest were two 2004 films about assisted suicide: *Million Dollar Baby*, which won the Academy Award for best picture, and *The Sea Inside*, which won the Academy Award for best foreign-language picture. Both films presented assisted death in a positive light.

In 2005 Martens was honoured by the Humanist Association of Canada with their Humanist of the Year Award, which was given to her by former winner Henry Morgentaler. In 2006 Martens was given the Marilyn Seguin award by the The World Federation of Right to Die Societies, an award given once every two years to the "person who has achieved much in her/his country for their national right-to-die movement."

After the Martens trial the CBC newsmagazine show *the fifth estate* announced that it was preparing to devote one entire program to the Martens case. I thought that this could be real breakthrough — something that might stir our politicians, finally, to act

I spoke several times to CBC representatives as they were preparing the program, and I expected a balanced and insightful look at the issues involved. Evelyn Martens risked her personal freedom to commit acts of human kindness, and I thought that something of this courage would be captured by the CBC. I imagined a storyline like that in *Vera Drake*, the great Mike Leigh movie that also came out in 2004, in which a (fictional) kindly older English woman performed illegal abortions for desperate English women who could get help nowhere else.

Many supporters of Martens hoped and expected that

the CBC documentary would tell her story in a sympathetic and understanding way, and perhaps help generate a groundswell to reexamine Canadian law on assisted death. However, the show, which aired on November 23, 2005, was a stunning disappointment.

The CBC producers chose not to tell the story of a courageous woman who risked her own freedom to help people in need. Instead, it was a story filled with distaste and incredulity: how could an apparently ordinary woman get involved in such an unsavoury business, and how did she manage to avoid conviction for her crimes? There was no analysis of the moral dilemma at the heart of the story — the problem of what to do when compassion and mercy conflict with the law. It is the dilemma of the underground railroad: do we help the wretched escape from their misery, or do we follow the law?

No sense, nothing whatever, of this central moral dilemma was brought forward in the show. Some think that the show and the negative portrayal it presented of Martens and what she had been doing had a cooling effect on progress toward changing Canadian law on assisted suicide — possibly slowing the momentum that was building toward more progressive legislation. The interest previously shown by the federal Liberals seemed suddenly to disappear.

The movement that many felt had started with the Martens trial seemed to dissipate.

The road to change in the law on assisted suicide was a long and rocky one, with many ups and downs. The impact that John Hofsess, Evelyn Martens, Sue Rodriguez and Robert Latimer had on public opinion was undoubtedly considerable. But the lull after Martens's trial was hard to understand; it had felt like something larger was about to happen. And then, in 2011, it suddenly did.

CHAPTER 6
A BREAKTHROUGH IN THE B.C. COURTS — 2012

By 2011 the public interest in a change in the law on assisted suicide again started to gain momentum. Parole Board slights to Robert Latimer continued to gain public attention. The experience of other countries revealed as groundless the fear that anything less than a prohibition of assistance in death would land us on a slippery slope to abusive treatment of the vulnerable in society. Justice Sopinka's interpretation of the *Charter*, in the Rodriguez case, fell further out of step with recent legal decisions. Other cases of assisted death further raised public concern.

In the fall of 2011 plans were afoot at the B.C. Civil Liberties Association (BCCLA) for a constitutional challenge of the assisted-suicide section of the *Criminal Code*. The case was heard by Justice Lynn Smith of the B.C. Supreme Court, in a number of hearings running from mid-November to mid-December 2011. The lead counsel for the plaintiffs was the formidable constitutional lawyer Joe Arvay.

In 1993 Arvay had almost become the lawyer for Sue Rodriguez as well. Even at that time Arvay was known for his efforts in seeking social justice. In the early days of the planning for the Rodriguez case, when philosopher Eike-Henner Kluge and John Hofsess were working out a legal strategy and before the involvement of Svend Robinson and lawyer Chris Considine, Hofsess met with Joe Arvay to sound him out on the possibility of having him take on the case. Arvay was intrigued, but because of other commitments at the time he could not do it.

Hofsess had intended to raise the money through a fundraising campaign centered on a televised "Concert for Sue," with the support of some famous entertainers. Considine, however, preferred to do the work pro bono, as he didn't want people to think that he would abandon Sue if funds were not raised to pay him.

The plaintiffs at the 2011 hearings included Lee Carter and her husband Hollis Johnson, who had helped Carter's mother, Kay, travel to Switzerland to get assistance in dying there. Switzerland is the only country that provides such a service for nonresidents. Kay Carter had been suffering from spinal stenosis, to the point where by summer of 2009 she required assistance for almost all of her daily activities. She could no longer hold a newspaper, change channels on the television or turn on the radio. She felt "trapped in her body and stripped of her independence." She felt that complete dependence and loss of control to be intolerable indignities.

In late July 2009, Kay decided she wanted to end her life by physician-assisted suicide, and she asked her daughter and son-in-law to help make the arrangements. They knew this would be very difficult in Canada, so the three of them began negotiations with the Swiss organization Dignitas. The planning for this was hard enough, because of the stress of Kay's impending death, but was made even harder because all of the arrangements had to be made in secret to avoid detection by Canadian authorities, who could construe the efforts being made as aiding or abetting suicide. Eventually, Lee, Hollis and two siblings went to Switzerland with Kay and were with her when she died. The total cost of all of this was $32,000, which came from the last of Kay's savings.

Because they aided and possibly abetted Kay Carter in ending her life, Lee and Hollis felt threatened by the Canadian law on assisted suicide, and they wanted protection that would come from a change in the law. Also, they felt that some day they themselves might become gravely ill and feel the need to end their own lives, and would like to be able to do so at home in the company of friends and relatives, without the expense and complications of arranging covert trips to Switzerland.

Another plaintiff was Gloria Taylor who, like Sue Rodriguez, suffered from ALS and did not want to live beyond the time when she would be completely disabled. Taylor had been showing symptoms for years, and in January 2010 was told by her neurologist that she would probably be paralyzed in six months and would likely die within a year. In fact, though, the disease progressed more slowly than that, and by the time of the hearings in late 2011 she was still able to move a little. Taylor stated in her affidavit:

> *I want to be very clear: I do not believe that my family considers me a burden. Nor am I concerned*

*that as I get more and more ill they will begin
to do so. When I told my family and friends that
I wanted a physician-assisted death, my concern
was that they might be disappointed in me for not
trying to hold on and stay with them until the last
possible moment. But I do want to express the fact
that I, myself, will be greatly distressed by living
in a state where I have no function or functionality
that requires others to attend to all of my needs
and thereby effectively oblige my family to bear
witness to the final steps of the process of my dying
with the indignity a slow death from ALS will
entail. I do not, in particular, want to be the cause
of my 11 year old granddaughter's sitting vigil
as I die an ugly death, and I believe that is what
she will do, because she loves me. I do not want to
be a burden, not because I fear my family does or
would resent me — I do not think that — rather,
I do not want to be a burden because I know they
love me . . .*

*I do not want my life to end violently. I do
not want my mode of death to be traumatic for
my family members. I want the legal right to die
peacefully, at the time of my own choosing, in the
embrace of my family and friends.*

*I know that I am dying, but I am far from
depressed. I have some down time — that is part
and parcel of the experience of knowing that you
are terminal. But there is still a lot of good in my
life; there are still things, like special times with
my granddaughter and family, that bring me
extreme joy. I will not waste any of my remaining*

time being depressed. I intend to get every bit of happiness I can wring from what is left of my life so long as it remains a life of quality; but I do not want to live a life without quality. There will come a point when I will know that enough is enough. I cannot say precisely when that time will be. It is not a question of "when I can't walk" or "when I can't talk". There is no pre-set trigger moment. I just know that, globally, there will be some point in time when I will be able to say — "this is it, this is the point where life is just not worthwhile". When that time comes, I want to be able to call my family together, tell them of my decision, say a dignified good-bye and obtain final closure — for me and for them.

My present quality of life is impaired by the fact that I am unable to say for certain that I will have the right to ask for physician-assisted dying when that "enough is enough" moment arrives. I live in apprehension that my death will be slow, difficult, unpleasant, painful, undignified and inconsistent with the values and principles I have tried to live by. I am proud to be dedicating the final days of my life trying to change the law in this respect. It is my hope that my actions in being a plaintiff in this case will bring others the peace of mind and sense of control that the law is presently denying me.

I am dying. I do not want to, but I am going to die; that is a fact. I can accept death because I recognize it as a part of life. What I fear is a death that negates, as opposed to concludes, my life. I do not want to die slowly, piece by piece. I do not want to waste away unconscious in a hospital bed. I do not want to die wracked with pain. It is very important to me that my family, and my granddaughter in particular, have final memories that capture me as I really am — not as someone I cannot identify with and have no desire to become.

I have pre-arranged my cremation. I have chosen songs I would like played at my service and am designing a memorial program. I am working on a eulogy, which my cousin has agreed to read aloud for me at the service. We create ourselves through our lives. These acts are part of my creation of the person I want to be and the person I want others to see and remember me as. I want my death to be part of that creation as well. As Sue Rodriguez asked before me — whose life is it anyway?

Gloria Taylor added that she found the idea of palliative sedation repugnant and did not view it an acceptable alternative to physician-assisted suicide.

A third plaintiff was Dr. William Shoichet, a family physician in Victoria who had treated many patients with terrible and irremediable illnesses who had suffered greatly because of those illnesses. This suffering included pain, humiliation at not being able to take care of basic needs, complete dependence on others and a severe loss of dignity and privacy. Dr. Shoichet would, in the right circumstances, be willing to carry out physician-assisted suicides if permitted to do so by the law.

Finally, the BCCLA was also a plaintiff because, as it was expressed by BCCLA Board member John Dixon, "it is critically important to have the involvement of an institutional litigant in *Charter* cases." Individuals may die or run out of money or for some other reason lose their commitment, but the BCCLA provides an institutional anchor for such cases.

Nineteen years after a similar appeal had been made on behalf of Sue Rodriguez, Joe Arvay, with a wealth of new evidence, was now on the case. And this time it was being heard by B.C. Supreme Court Justice Lynn Smith. The defendants were the Attorneys General of Canada and of British Columbia. Lead counsel for the former was Donnaree Nygard, and for the latter George H. Copley. Copley was assisted by Craig E. Jones.

Oddly, as the constitutional challenge was taking shape, Jones made what appeared to be a threatening gesture toward those pushing for such a challenge. The Farewell Foundation claimed that on October 3, 2011, Jones, as an agent of the B.C. Attorney General's office, issued a notice that he intended to seek an order requiring that all persons who know the details of, or have participated in, instances of assisted suicide in Canada must be named, with their addresses, and listed for the Attorney General (AG).

Was this an effort to intimidate those who wanted to change the law? It seemed strangely out of place, especially since by this time it seemed clear that Canadian society was moving toward a more progressive stance on end-of-life issues — some sort of constitutional challenge was likely coming, and it would probably lead to some softening of the Canadian stance on assisted suicide. But the B.C. Attorney General chose to respond with this request to all people who might have known anything about an assisted suicide — a request that undoubtedly would seem threatening to most such people. The list the AG's office was seeking might have given them grounds for prosecution for those who responded. This was a very strange request on the eve of a major constitutional challenge on the issue.

Jones claimed that the request for a list was simply to put before the court all "necessary and relevant evidence," but I doubt that anyone saw it as just that. And such a mild purpose was hardly consistent with the aggressive tone of Jones's request. He said he was prepared to subpoena lawyers of the BCCLA, forcing them to disclose the identity of one person who had allegedly participated in the deaths of both of his parents.

Joe Arvay's response? "Bring it on."

At the urging of Justice Lynn Smith, Jones and the Attorney General's office dropped the request for names as the case proceeded. Justice Smith herself was a paragon of reason and of compassion in her handling of the hearings and in writing her judgment, and gave a detailed, thorough and insightful analysis of every aspect of the case, not just from a legal perspective but from a caring and compassionate one as well.

Smith was born and raised in Calgary, earning an Honours BA in Philosophy from the University of Calgary in 1967 and an LLB from the University of British Columbia in 1973. In 2004 she was given an Honorary Doctorate of Law by Simon Fraser University. She had a distinguished career as a lawyer and as an academic, spending sixteen years as a member of the University of British Columbia Law School, including six years as Dean of the Faculty. In 1992 she was named Queen's Counsel and in 1998 she was appointed to be a Justice of Supreme Court of British Columbia. She has many publications and many honours for the work she has done. Her husband, Justice Jon Sigurdson, also sits on the B.C. Supreme Court.

The task ahead of Smith was a very difficult and challenging one. She had the compelling statements from the plaintiffs, she had the grumbly attitudes of the two attorney-general offices, she had detailed presentations by several interveners and she had to absorb twenty-four days of detailed testimony, including that of fifty-seven expert witnesses (thirty-nine for the plaintiffs and eighteen for the AGs). Then there were many reports of relevant commissions and many other documents that required careful examination.

The first issue to be resolved was to determine if there was sufficient reason to revisit this end-of-life issue that supposedly was settled in the Rodriguez case. Once the Court decides on an issue, that's usually the end of the matter. Lower courts are generally bound by that decision, good or bad, and the Supreme Court of Canada (SCC) will not generally look at any particular issue again, unless it can be shown that circumstances since the original ruling have significantly changed.

The legal principle involved here is called *stare decisis*, which means what's settled is settled. There is a general assumption (not always true) that the court that made a decision, especially the SCC, knew what it was doing. This attitude is reflected in the power of precedent in legal decisions. The Attorneys General claimed that the Rodriguez decision had decided upon end-of-life matters — essentially that it was too dangerous to allow any sort of assisted death — and that there was no justification for going back over this settled territory.

That, then, was the first challenge of Joe Arvay and his team — to try to get a reconsideration of the Rodriguez decision. They had some compelling arguments to present to support lifting the ban on assisted suicide but, even so, if the circumstances were deemed to be much the same as they were twenty years earlier in the Rodriguez case, then precedent would rule.

That decision made by the Court in the Rodriguez case had been a life-altering blow to many thousands of Canadians. It drastically set back social progress on this issue, causing us to fall behind developments in other countries. This situation could have been avoided if just one more judge had been persuaded to vote for Rodriguez. Now our Attorneys General were arguing, in effect, that this narrow decision should stand forever.

Arvay had to give reasons why the matter should be reopened. He had to argue that circumstances had changed significantly since 1993. For one thing, public opinion seemed to have shifted considerably, with something like 64% of Canadians (even higher in some polls) in favour of some form of assisted suicide. Comparable figures from 1993 are not available, but Justice Sopinka, in his majority opinion in *Rodriguez*, had claimed that the lack of public support was one reason for his decision. However, if this ever had been a valid reason for opposing assisted suicide, it no longer was so.

Another claim made in the 1993 decision was that no other country had legalized assisted suicide, and this too was used to justify his ruling. But again circumstances had radically changed by 2012, with a number of countries having adopted legislation allowing some form of assisted suicide and in some cases even euthanasia.

Another of the key points in the decision was that even if the Canadian assisted suicide law was discriminatory, and a violation of Section 15 of the *Charter*, the risks of permitting assistance in suicide were too great: that the weak and vulnerable might be victimized and pushed into dying prematurely. The Court found that safeguards would be insufficient and, since at the time no other countries were allowing assisted suicide, there was no way to get evidence corroborating or opposing the claim. But now, in 2012, there was extensive evidence, exhaustively reviewed by Justice Smith, that safeguards do work.

There had been another significant development as well. Sopinka in the Supreme Court decision had made much of the idea of the sanctity of life and that preservation of human life must outweigh all other considerations. But that rigid view has probably always been a minority one, with sources in religious teachings, and was apparently no longer held even by the Attorney General of B.C. Following the Rodriguez case in 1993, it has been official policy in B.C. that decisions on laying charges "will be made on a case by case basis following an examination of the facts and circumstances of each case," when the motivation for ending a life has been compassion for another person. Two requirements for prosecution are specified:

1.   there must be a substantial likelihood of conviction, and
2.   prosecution must be seen to be in the public interest.

The policy also specifies that palliative sedation, even if it hastens death, is not subject to criminal prosecution, and neither is withholding or withdrawing treatment causing death.

It was pointed out by Arvay that this policy in B.C. allows for prosecutorial discretion in regard to cases of assisted suicide, thus contradicting the principle of the absolute sanctity of life stated in the 1993 decision.

Taken together, all of these factors justified, to Smith, the reopening of the 1993 Supreme Court decision on assisted death.

* * *

There were many highlights in Smith's ruling, far too many to recount in this brief summary. She provides insightful commentary on the question about valuing human life, quoting one of the expert witnesses, Professor Wane Sumner:

> *Normally we assume that death is one of the worst fates that can befall us, which is why in both ethics and law the causing of death is taken to be such a serious matter. But what makes death such a bad thing in the normal case is what it takes away from us — the continuation of a life worth living. The disvalue of death is therefore a direct function of the value of the life thereby lost. This is the deprivation account of the badness of death: death is bad for us by virtue of depriving us of the goods of continued life. On this account showing that death would be bad for a person requires a comparison between two possible futures for that person: the one in which he dies and the one in which he lives on. If the goods of further life would outweigh the evils then it would be better for the person to continue living, and death would*

therefore be a harm to him since it would deprive
him of this good future.

In response to the often-made claim that if physician-assisted suicide is available then family members will encourage this in order, for example, to get faster access to their inheritance, Smith comments on the research carried out in Oregon by one of expert witnesses for the plaintiffs:

> *In one of Dr. Ganzini's studies, she found that in many cases a patient's decision to obtain a lethal prescription was influenced by family. She stated under cross-examination, however, that these were predominantly cases of the family influencing the patient not to die. She also testified that in her experience the patients seeking hastened death are highly independent people who are expressing their life-long values, while their families are expressing a wish to have the chance, for once, to take care of them.*

In regard to another frequently expressed concern about physician-assisted suicide, that the disabled will be particularly vulnerable to being abused by such a practice, Smith writes:

> *. . . there is no evidence that persons with disabilities are at heightened risk of accessing physician-assisted dying in jurisdictions where it is permitted . . . I accept that persons with disabilities face prejudice and stereotyping and that there is a risk of unconscious bias about the quality of life of a person with a*

disability. However . . . I am not persuaded that
the risks to persons with disabilities are such that
they cannot be avoided through practices of careful
and well-informed capacity assessments by qualified
physicians who are alert to those risks.

Smith's ruling, all 1,415 articles of it, is full of clear, reasonable and insightful comments. Her rulings, derived from her observations and analyses were concise and clear, and are summarized here:

The plaintiffs succeed in their Charter *challenge*
of Section 241(b), prohibiting assisted suicide, of
the Criminal Code of Canada.
    The law will become invalid in one year (giving
legislators time to draft a new law) but in the
meantime Gloria Taylor will be allowed the option
of physician-assisted suicide.

PROPOSED CANADIAN ASSISTED SUICIDE PROCEDURE

Justice Smith, in her ruling, quoted Arvay and his team on safeguards that could be incorporated into legislation. Such safeguards, Arvay argued, would satisfy all reasonable concerns in regard to physician-assisted suicide. The arguments are summarized as follows:

1) Assessing Competency

A mandatory psychiatric evaluation for informed consent should be carried out at the highest degree of scrutiny, with due consideration of all relevant information, and involving more than one interview with the patient if, in the assessing psychiatrist's opinion, more than one interview is appropriate.

There should be disqualification of individuals actively suffering from a major depressive disorder.

There should be a requirement that any death by physician-assisted suicide take place after a certain minimum waiting period, following psychiatric approval of the patient's decision-making capacity.

2) Voluntariness

There should be a requirement for a formal written request and a requirement for repeated requests.

There should be a minimum waiting period (which might vary by category of medical condition and might, for example, provide for a longer waiting period when a patient has only recently acquired a disabling condition) to ensure the enduring and persistent nature of the request.

Patients should have the option of refusal made available throughout the process, by requiring the patient to positively confirm his or her wishes to a person with no possible investment in the outcome of the process, such as a confidential patient advocate, at all key stages of the process.

There should be a requirement that a representative of a government agency attend as a witness prior to any death, in order to confirm the continuing voluntariness at the time of death.

3) Limiting Access to Euthanasia

A further safeguard would be provided if euthanasia were only available in circumstances where the patient was incapable of committing suicide without assistance.

4) Being Fully Informed

The patient must be fully informed by the treating physician as to his or her condition and treatment options, including, but not limited to, palliative care options.

This must be confirmed by an independent physician who is qualified by expertise or experience regarding the patient's illness, and who has examined the patient and reviewed the patient's relevant medical records.

The patient should have a palliative care consultation with a physician who has expertise in palliative care; and the patient must be advised of the risks associated with physician-assisted dying, including any risk factors related to the medication to be used.

5) Eligibility Determination

Patients getting assistance in dying should be grievously and irremediably ill and suffering intolerably as a result of a medical condition.

The illness must be without remedy, as determined by treatment options acceptable to the patient; and must be causing enduring physical, psychological or psychosocial suffering that:

1.   is intolerable to that person, and
2.   cannot be alleviated by treatment options acceptable to that person.

6) Procedural Reporting

The physician and second physician must each be required to provide a report to an expert review panel that must consist of an ethicist, a lawyer and a doctor.

The members of the expert review panel must, within

forty-eight hours of receiving the reports, review them for accuracy and adequacy of information, and indicate whether they approve of the reports as provided.

The decision of the expert review panel will be subject to appeal by the patient directly to the provincial Superior Court.

* * *

Smith's ruling, after decades of public concern about the restrictions on assisting death, constituted a dramatic breakthrough. Finally there was a definitive court ruling that took on, directly, all of the worries and fears about assisted death, and countered them with evidence and impeccable logic. Never again would it be possible for the slippery-slope argument to have so much force: no such slope had materialized in countries where assisted death was allowed. Evidence trumped speculation. Fact over-turned fiction. Events had progressed to the point where no longer could frightening claims about the consequences of relaxing the laws against assisted death be regarded as convincing, at least by those willing to look carefully at the experience in other jurisdictions. Even claims about the sanctity of life had been rendered moot by the Attorney General's own policies.

Of course, Smith's ruling was not the end of the story. There were appeals to go through, with the matter eventually ending up back at the Supreme Court of Canada. In the meantime, eloquent voices from across the country continued to speak in favour of progressive change. And Quebec, often the most socially progressive province in Canada, took its own steps to try to circumvent the regressive Canadian law on assisted death.

CHAPTER 7
SOME DOCTORS WEIGH IN — 2013

DONALD LOW

The medical community has long had mixed feelings about assisted death. Some doctors claim that helping a patient die is a violation of the Hippocratic injunction to "do no harm," because death is the ultimate harm. Other doctors have looked at the idea of harm in a more nuanced way — that harm includes allowing a patient to needlessly suffer from terminal illness. One of these, Dr. Donald Low of Toronto, spoke out on the topic, as he himself was about to die.

Dr. Low had gained fame in 2003 for his battle against the SARS outbreak; he was the microbiologist-in-chief at Mount Sinai Hospital in Toronto at the time. SARS, severe acute respiratory syndrome, was first detected in mainland China in 2002, but the government of the People's Republic of China was slow to report the disease to the World Health

Organization. Soon SARS spread to Hong Kong and then to Vietnam. By mid-March 2003 a global alert about this new infectious disease was issued. Cases were reported in Singapore and Thailand. Within days it was reported in the US and then in Canada. It became clear that the disease, whatever it was, was being spread by air travel.

By April 13, 2003, thirteen people in Canada had died from the disease, but the good news was that researchers at the Michael Smith Genome Sciences Centre of the B.C. Cancer Agency had identified the virus that was causing the disease. By January 2004, the outbreak had ended, with forty-four people in Canada having died. There have been no cases since. Over eight hundred people had been infected in China, with close to 10% of them dying.

Donald Low had previously become well known as an expert on necrotizing fasciitis (flesh eating disease) and was an early advocate for the prudent use of antibiotics, to prevent the development of resistant strains of bacteria.

When the SARS epidemic hit Canada, microbiologist Low found himself at the centre of the outbreak of this new infectious disease — a very demanding and grim task. He assumed an unofficial leadership role by calmly talking to the public in a knowledgeable and reassuring manner. Low had to go into quarantine at one point, because of exposure to an infected colleague, but he emerged two weeks later, unscathed. He later was hired to revitalize Ontario's public health laboratory, which had been criticized by a commission of enquiry.

Low faced another difficult but more personal health crisis when, in early 2013, he was diagnosed as having a brain tumour. He was sixty-eight at the time. Some months earlier he had been bothered by a roaring sound in his ears, but tests had been inconclusive. Then, as symptoms worsened, he had a CT scan that revealed an inoperable tumour. He tried some treatments, including chemotherapy and radiation, but nothing helped much and the tumour continued to grow. His wife, Maureen Taylor, formerly a medical reporter for the CBC, says she regrets having him take the treatments, which made his precious remaining days more difficult.

Low did not want to deteriorate to a point where he became totally dependent; he did not want to reach the stage where he had no control over his body. Taylor says that he was not suicidal or depressed; he just wanted to avoid the final stages of his illness. They thought about flying to Switzerland where aid in dying is legal and available to foreigners, but Low wanted to stay at home with his family around him.

Low and Taylor thought about various ways of ending his life, but without the availability of anyone to help the choices all seemed difficult. Low did receive excellent palliative care and stayed relatively comfortable as his health declined. Finally he decided that since it was unclear to him and his wife how he might best hasten death, he would just stop eating food and drinking water.

Then, eight days before he died, Low made a heart-wrenching video pleading with the government of Canada to relax its laws on assisted suicide. He was breathing heavily in the video but he was perfectly clear and rational. A piece of tape held open his left eye, as he had lost control over the muscles of his eyelids. The video was not released until after he died.

Low started by introducing himself and explaining that had he been diagnosed as having a brain stem tumour in

February 2013. It had been a terrible thing to hear because, as an internist himself, he knew the prognosis was bad. But he had been able to handle the news with some equanimity, worrying mainly about having to tell his family.

Low said he was fortunate in that he had not had pain or much paralysis yet, although he knew those things would come. "I'm worried about how it's going to end; I know it's never going to get better. I'm going to die and what worries me is how I am going to die."

Low was concerned about having to be carried from "bathroom to bed" and about how he would soon have difficulty in swallowing. He agreed that palliative care was important, but it could do little to relieve the symptoms he was about to endure. Palliative care could make his condition a little easier to face, but could not take his expected discomfort away.

When Low and his wife first realized that his condition was terminal they looked into alternatives for dying, but they were surprised by the obstacles that existed in Canada. There was no place where one could have support for "dying with dignity," as there is in some parts of the world. Low talked of being given a narcotic and then falling asleep in the presence of his family, but such a thing was difficult in Canada — both getting the necessary drugs and having others present, who might then be prosecuted.

Low talked about how he thought it would be long time before Canada matures to the point where we accept dying with dignity. He said there is a lot of opposition, especially from some clinicians.

"I wish they could live in my body for twenty-four hours," he said, "and I think they would change their opinion. I'm just frustrated at not being able to have control over my own life."

He said he envied people in countries like Switzerland and the Netherlands, where help in dying was much more easily obtained. He said:

> *Why make people suffer for no reason when there is an alternative? I just don't understand it. My hope is that I'll die a painless death, that ideally I would go to sleep one night and I would not wake up in the morning . . . I'm not afraid of dying. I could make that decision tomorrow. I just do not want to be in a long protracted process where I'm unable to carry out my normal bodily functions and talk with my family and enjoy the last few days of my life. The fear is that that is not going to happen.*

Low died eight days later of natural causes, and then his video was posted online.

In September of 2013, shortly after the Low video was released, the CBC reported that a spokesperson for the Justice Minister sent them an email stating that the government had "no intention" of reopening the debate on the laws surrounding euthanasia and assisted suicide.

However, a year later Low's wife, Maureen Taylor, was able to say at a news conference in Toronto:

> *I'm still grieving for my husband and think I will be for my whole life. But I can say with certainty that Don would be most encouraged and surprised at the discussion and the movement that's taken place on the issue of assisted suicide.*

THE CANADIAN MEDICAL ASSOCIATION SOFTENS ITS OPPOSITION

While individual doctors such as Donald Low often spoke of the need for more progressive end-of-life legislation, the Canadian Medical Association (CMA) had, for decades, been opposed to physician-assisted death. Justice Sopinka used this justification in his majority opinion in the 1993 Sue Rodriguez case:

> *I also place some significance in the fact that the official position of various medical associations is against decriminalizing assisted suicide (Canadian Medical Association, British Medical Association, Council of Ethical and Judicial Affairs of the American Medical Association, World Medical Association and the American Nurses Association). Given the concerns about abuse that have been expressed and the great difficulty in creating appropriate safeguards to prevent these, it can not be said that the blanket prohibition on assisted suicide is arbitrary or unfair, or that it is not reflective of fundamental values at play in our society. I am thus unable to find that any principle of fundamental justice is violated by s. 241 (b).*

The matter arose again in the B.C. Supreme Court's 2012 ruling to decriminalize assisted suicide, although the CMA's position was not a determining factor in the ruling there. Justice Smith allowed that at the time the CMA was strongly against physician-assisted suicide and euthanasia. In Section 274 of her ruling, Smith quoted extensively from the then most recent (2007) CMA statement on the matter:

. . . Euthanasia and assisted suicide, as understood here, must be distinguished from the withholding or withdrawal of inappropriate, futile or unwanted medical treatment or the provision of compassionate palliative care, even when these practices shorten life. The CMA does not support euthanasia or assisted suicide. It urges its members to uphold the principles of palliative care. . .

. . . Euthanasia and assisted suicide are opposed by almost every national medical association and prohibited by the law codes of almost all countries. A change in the legal status of these practices in Canada would represent a major shift in social policy and behaviour. For the medical profession to support such a change and subsequently participate in these practices, a fundamental reconsideration of traditional medical ethics would be required . . .

. . . Canadian physicians should not participate in euthanasia or assisted suicide.

The document went on to list concerns of the CMA about any changes in the law on assisted suicide and euthanasia. Palliative care should first be improved; suicide prevention programs should be maintained and strengthened. A study of decision-making by doctors during their dealing with dying patients should be undertaken. The public should be given adequate opportunity to comment on proposed legislation. Legislators should be sure that the process can be controlled.

Justice Smith acknowledged the CMA's firm position and cautious approach to change, but pointed out that many CMA members did not agree with the Association on this, nor did a number of other medical organizations.

Interestingly, Eike-Henner Kluge, the philosopher from the University of Victoria mentioned elsewhere in this book, was founding Director of Ethics and Legal Affairs for the CMA in 1989. Kluge had intended to develop a much more progressive position on assisted death for the CMA, but he left the organization before getting a chance to do so. After he left, it took until 2014 for a new position to be taken by the CMA:

> . . . *The CMA supports patients' access to the full spectrum of end of life care that is legal in Canada. The CMA supports the right of all physicians, within the bounds of existing legislation, to follow their conscience when deciding whether to provide medical aid in dying as defined in this policy.*

This key clause was overwhelmingly approved at a meeting of the CMA General Council in October of 2014, following an earlier approval at the annual CMA meeting the previous August. This new policy, following this radical change, was rewritten and approved on December 18, 2014. It will probably undergo further changes, so has not been fully included here.

One point perhaps should be made, in the hope that if further changes are made it will be clarified. For some reason, in its definition of euthanasia the CMA does not draw a distinction between voluntary, non-voluntary and involuntary euthanasia (with consent, without consent and contrary to the wishes of the patient). Perhaps the CMA saw no point in making this distinction, because when they wrote their new policy they were opposed to all forms of euthanasia. But the issue will likely emerge from the CMA membership. Many, including this author, argue that there is no real moral distinction between physician-assisted suicide and voluntary euthanasia, and that legalizing one and criminalizing the other makes no logical sense. So the issue will arise and it would be helpful in the definitions to clarify these distinctions.

I should perhaps comment also on the CMA's adamant declaration in the new document that palliative sedation is "NOT euthanasia or physician-assisted death." (Emphasis in the original.) Clearly the CMA would have it so, because palliative sedation is routinely practiced by many of its members; but, as is discussed in more detail in Appendix 3, such a declaration does not make it so. This entirely unregulated practice, that almost surely in some cases at least leads to shortening of life, strikes me as much more problematic than a regulated system of assisted suicide and euthanasia.

Apparently there was some rancorous debate about the new CMA policy. One reporter, André Picard of the *Globe and Mail*, speaking about an earlier CMA policy convention in Calgary in August of 2013, said that:

> *physicians got bogged down on semantics, in lengthy discussions about the appropriate language to use to describe hastening death at the end of life, and deferred real debate to a later unspecified date and another unspecified time. In short, fear prevailed . . . fear of exposing the deep, deep divisions in the medical profession.*

Then, in August of 2014 the CMA held its annual meeting in Ottawa, with euthanasia and assisted suicide on the agenda. That is when delegates voted strongly in favour of "the right of all physicians, within the bounds of existing legislation, to follow their conscience when deciding whether to provide medical aid in dying." As noted, on December 18, 2014, the change in perspective was made explicit in the revised policy. There was no longer any statement to the effect that the CMA was opposed to assisted suicide and euthanasia. But the CMA continued to grapple with the issue and was unable to come to an agreed position.

CHAPTER 8

WHOSE JURISDICTION IS IT ANYWAY? QUEBEC — 2014

Is assisted death a health care matter or is it a criminal one? This may seem an odd question, but in the contentious and confusing world of federal-provincial jurisdictional responsibilities, it is significant. If assisted death is a criminal matter, then it properly can be governed by the *Criminal Code of Canada*, which makes assisted suicide a criminal offence with a penalty of up to fourteen years in prison. But if assisted death is deemed a health care matter then it comes under provincial jurisdiction; and provinces, like Quebec, can make the relevant laws.

Provincial jurisdiction over health arises from the *Constitutional Act* of 1867, which states that each provincial legislature "may exclusively make laws" in designated areas. One of those areas, specified in Clause 92.7, concerns the "Establishment, Maintenance and Management of

Hospitals." This has been interpreted to mean that while the federal government retains some involvement in certain issues related to health, actual health care is a provincial responsibility. This interpretation of this distinction is crucial in determining who has jurisdiction in cases of assisted suicide. Quebec asserted jurisdiction in this area with the passage of Bill 52, legislation concerning end-of-life care that permits, in certain circumstances, physician-assisted death.

The Supreme Court of Canada has held that the federal government does have broad powers in regard to health and criminal law, as well as some control over health spending and other matters such as health research and disease prevention and control. This legal power includes general concerns about public health such as cigarettes, drugs and food regulation, radiation-emitting devices and many others.

So where does assisted suicide fall? Quebec argues that in severe cases of distress at the end of life, assisted suicide is simply an extension of the delivery of health care services. Quebec has strong legal support for its position. The federal government has opposed the idea on the grounds that it alone has the right to make laws like these, including in areas related to health.

On December 4, 2009, following a recommendation by the Quebec College of Physicians, the Quebec National Assembly voted to create a committee to look into "dying with dignity" and how it could be put into practice. The motion had been brought forward by Véronique Hivon, Member of the National Assembly (MNA) from the opposition Parti Québécois. Over the next two years the committee met with thirty-two knowledgeable people, received over three hundred position papers, reviewed sixty-six hundred answers to an online questionnaire, held public meetings in eight cities and sent a delegation to France, Belgium and the Netherlands to investigate assisted-suicide practices in those countries. During this time a Provincial election was called and the ruling Liberals were narrowly defeated by the Parti Québécois, led by Pauline Marois

The committee presented its findings on March 22, 2012, making twenty-four recommendations, which included support for physician-assisted dying. In June the Quebec Department of Justice consulted a panel of seventeen legal experts, who supported the idea of the proposed legislation. So did new Premier Marois. She asked Hivon, who had made the original motion, to explore the matter and to draft legislation. On June 12, 2013, Hivon tabled Bill 52.

Over the next few months public hearings were held about the new bill, and on October 29 the National Assembly approved the bill in principle by an eighty-four to twenty-six vote.

This extraordinarily thorough process continued with the Health and Human Services Committee of the National Assembly reviewing each clause of the bill and making fifty-seven amendments. In February of 2014 the National Assembly began debate on the bill, and on June 5 it was passed by a vote of ninety-four to twenty-two, this time by a re-elected Liberal government.

The right-wing federal Conservative Party government of Stephen Harper was undoubtedly looking askance at this movement in Quebec. Physician-assisted suicide was definitely not on their agenda, but now they had this formidable challenge from Quebec, as well as growing unrest on the issue elsewhere in Canada. Not only was there an impending legal battle with Quebec, there was the B.C. Supreme Court

146 THE RIGHT TO DIE

decision in 2012 in the Carter case (see Chapter 6) and the Supreme Court of Canada's impending decision on the matter. This matter was handled seriously and thoughtfully in Quebec, with members of both parties working together to address and deal with a problem of serious concern to many of their constituents. It is striking to see Quebec lead the nation in social progress. It is puzzling because a higher portion of Quebec's population identifies itself as Catholic, and the Catholic Church of course is strongly opposed to any sort of intentional human death.

There were voices of dissent at the hearing in Quebec. The ubiquitous Euthanasia Prevention Coalition (EPC) was, of course, there. Its position, that "euthanasia is homicide and not health care," obviously supported the disputed federal position that Quebec was bound by the federal law making assisted suicide a crime. The EPC argued as well that the existing laws are protective, not discriminatory; that safeguards are being abused in other countries; that the issues should be settled in Parliament not the courts; that there is no constitutional right to die; and that legalizing these matters diminishes personal autonomy by "empowering doctors to end lives of patients at the most vulnerable time of their lives."

The opening statement in the explanatory notes for Bill 52 read:

> *The purpose of this Act is to ensure that end-of-life patients are provided care that is respectful of their dignity and their autonomy and to recognize the primacy of wishes expressed freely and clearly with respect to end-of-life care.*

The Quebec legislation had three main components: to set guidelines for physician-assisted dying, to set protocols for palliative sedation and to expand palliative care.

Physician-Assisted Dying

The bill referred to "medical aid in dying," defined as "care consisting in the administration by a physician of medications or substances to an end-of-life patient, at the patient's request, in order to relieve their suffering by hastening death." This bill is especially notable because, by using the term "medical aid in dying" instead of "medical aid in suicide," it allows for voluntary euthanasia, where the final action can be taken by a doctor. If it allowed only assisted suicide then the patient would have to take the final step. Most dying people prefer voluntary euthanasia, as shown in the Netherlands, where both are available. It is favoured there by a ratio of about twenty-three to one over assisted suicide.

If the Quebec law holds up to the inevitable legal challenges, the hastening of death for a suffering person with a terminal illness will be viewed, in Quebec, as a desirable and humane extension of medical care.

In December of 2015 the Quebec Supreme Court approved *Bill 52*, and plans are now afoot for the matter to proceed. It remains to be seen if the Supreme Court of Canada will make a jurisdictional challenge.

* * *

To receive aid in dying, Bill 52 specified that the patient must:

1. be insured under the *Health Act*;
2. be of full age and capable of giving consent;

3. be at the end of life;
4. suffer from an incurable illness;
5. be in an advanced state of irreversible decline in capability; and
6. experience constant and unbearable physical or psychological suffering that cannot be relieved in a manner the patient deems tolerable.

Patients must also request this aid in dying themselves, "in a free and informed manner," using a prescribed form dated and signed. This signed form must be witnessed and countersigned by a health or social services professional.

If a person cannot physically sign the form a third capable person may do so, but not a member of the attending medical team. The patient then may at any time withdraw his or her request, or ask that it be put off.

Before proceeding, the physician has several conditions that must be met. The physician must:

1. ensure that all the conditions for the patient are met, and ensure that the request is being made freely and without external pressure, that the patient is properly informed about their illness, that the claim of persistent suffering is valid, that the desire to die is consistent over reasonably spaced intervals, that the patient's situation has been discussed with other members of the care team and, if the patient agrees, with close relatives;
2. ensure the patient has had the chance to discuss their request with other persons they may wish to talk to; and

3.   obtain the opinion of a second independent physician confirming that all criteria have been met.

If all these conditions are met, then the attending physician must oversee the treatment personally and stay with the patient until he or she dies.

A further safeguard is provided by the requirement that reports be filed with hospital authorities on all assisted deaths taking place there, and that the Collège des Médecins du Québec prepare an annual report on assisted deaths taking place in private institutions.

All of these new practices are put under the purview of a commission on end-of-life care (the Commission), to be established with eleven members appointed by the provincial government. The Commission is to include health and social service professionals, chosen in consultation with various agencies, two legal professionals and an ethicist from a university. The report is to be made public.

The Commission's mandate is to "examine any matter relating to end-of-life care," including evaluating the implementation of Bill 52, making recommendations for change to the government and preparing reports every year and then overview reports every five years.

Under the bill a physician and/or any other health professional can refuse to participate in assisted dying because of personal convictions. Nevertheless, such reluctant persons must ensure that others, willing to follow the wishes of the patient, take their place.

Advance medical directives, by a person capable of giving consent, may be used to give or withhold regular medical care once the patient becomes incapable of giving consent, but cannot be used to authorize assistance in dying.

PALLIATIVE CARE AND PALLIATIVE SEDATION

Palliative care is defined in Bill 52 as care provided to a dying person to "relieve their suffering, without delaying or hastening death" and to "maintain the best quality of life possible and provide them and their close relations with the support they need."

This is not at all controversial, except that such care is not universally available. Bill 52 supported strengthening such care.

Palliative sedation, however, sometimes called terminal sedation, is another matter. Bill 52 opted, for clarity, to use the term "continuous palliative sedation," by which is meant "administering medications or substances to an end-of-life patient to relieve their suffering by rendering them unconscious until death ensues."

Bill 52 had only two clauses on palliative sedation out of a total of seventy-eight. It said that the patient (or acceptable designate) must give consent and must be informed about the nature of the sedation — that they will not be waking up. The consent must not be made as a result of external pressure. Consent must be in writing, which a third person can provide if necessary.

Only these two clauses were needed to deal with this matter because the bill, in legalizing assisted death, resolved the controversial aspect of palliative sedation: that in some cases this treatment hastens death. Therefore it can reasonably be viewed as assisting suicide or, more accurately, as voluntary euthanasia. But if assisted death is legalized, the point becomes moot — hastening death by prescribed means would be legal. For more discussion of palliative sedation see Appendix 3.

* * *

So, as of June 2014, Canada had one province passing carefully vetted legislation permitting assisted death. Earlier, in 2012, the B.C. Supreme Court had struck down the federal law banning assisted suicide. Both of these decisions required validation by the Supreme Court of Canada, but it was evident that acceptance of the idea of assisted death in Canada was moving along quickly. In unprecedented actions, one provincial legislature and one provincial Supreme Court had legalized assisted death, or at least tried to do so. The momentum for change now was very considerable.

In the interlude between these judicial and legislative actions and the Canadian Supreme Court's hearing on the matter, in the fall of 2014, yet another powerful public statement supporting assisted death was made by another dying person, this time by Gillian Bennett, wife of eminent philosopher Jonathan Bennett.

CHAPTER 9
GILLIAN BENNETT, DEAD AT NOON — 2014

Sometimes inspiration for more progressive legislation on assisted death comes from influential public figures such as Dr. Donald Low. Other times it has come from ordinary citizens who find the strength to make movingly eloquent statements on the matter in their final days.

At noon on August 18, 2014, eighty-three-year-old Gillian Bennett, of Bowen Island in British Columbia, took her own life. In the next several days her story was carried in the news media across the country. It was an unusual suicide, which explains the media coverage.

Most suicides are unhappy acts of desperation — events that compassionate observers would try to prevent, if they only knew how to do so. Suicide prevention services do important work in trying to stop these premature endings of lives, lives that still offer the possibility of hope and happiness. Still, there are ten suicides each day in Canada; ten personal decisions, disproportionately amongst the minorities and the poor, that represent tragic failures of our social systems.

But then there are some few suicides that are not tragic events but, rather, are welcome relief from suffering and the indignity of continuing to live inside a hopelessly compromised body. In such instances the unpleasantness of continued life can be far worse than a peaceful death. Then the compassionate response is the opposite to that suggested above: people in such distress, without hope for improvement, should be given whatever assistance they need in undertaking the grave and often difficult task of ending their suffering and their indignity.

Gillian Bennett's suicide was one of this latter kind, made particularly notable by the remarkable letter she wrote and arranged to make public after she died.

* * *

Growing up in the 1930s in Christchurch, New Zealand, young Mary Gillian Quentin-Baxter attended a girl's school and then in 1949 went to Canterbury College, where through the French Club she encountered a very bright fellow student, Jonathan Bennett. They became friends. Jonathan was enrolled in a liberal arts program with the intention of going into medicine, but was "kidnapped" by philosophy. In the progress of his studies, still preparing for medicine, he spent a year taking science courses. But he realized then that he was unhappy with the direction in which he was headed. He did not really like zoology and the other science courses. He liked philosophy. He missed it and soon returned to it.

Gillian was also taking philosophy, though not in the same classes as Jonathan, who had started college two years before she did. She studied philosophy not so much because she was as deeply interested in it as was Jonathan, but because she much admired one of the professors in the department, Arthur Norman Prior, a widely known and influential logician. Jonathan and Gillian went on to take degrees in philosophy, and both became longtime friends with Prior, who died in 1969. Their paths would cross again in Oxford, England.

Jonathan graduated in 1952 and went to Oxford for two years while Gillian, graduating a year later, went to Oxford herself in 1955, just as Jonathan was going off to the United States. He then returned to Oxford for the summer of 1956 and, by either good luck or good management, or both, they found themselves in the same place at the same time. Jonathan had always fancied Gillian but they had spent the immediately preceding years in different parts of the world. But now they were finally in the same place at the same time.

As it happened, their former teacher Arthur Prior was also in Oxford that year, as a visiting professor, and he provided a stretcher in the living room of his Oxford apartment for Jonathan to sleep on. Gillian was staying just a hundred yards down the road. The two began to spend a lot of time together, forming a bond that would stay intact until noontime, August 18, 2014 — until death did them part.

During their time together in the summer of 1956 Jonathan began to feel very strongly that he wanted to marry Gillian; he could not imagine marrying anyone else. He could not get her out of his mind. He proposed and they were married in Cambridge later that same year, at

Magdalene College, with Robert Runcie presiding; Runcie later became the Archbishop of Canterbury.

For the next twelve years Jonathan was a lecturer at Cambridge. Gillian taught in a school in the town of Cambridge for short while after they were married, but then gave up teaching as they had their first child, Sara, within a year and then their second, Guy, about a year and a half after that.

In 1968 Jonathan was offered the headship of the philosophy department in a new university in Vancouver — Simon Fraser University. These were radical times, however, especially at Simon Fraser, with all sorts of student and faculty unrest: occupations of buildings, protest marches and demands for "democratization" of the university. Jonathan was never comfortable there and decided to move on after three years.

Jonathan and Gillian very much liked Vancouver, however, and wanted to stay there. They regarded it as a "northern hemisphere substitute" for their beloved New Zealand, with its mountains and seacoast and moderate climate. And they wanted their children to stay in school in British Columbia. Jonathan was offered a position across the city at the University of British Columbia, where he spent the next nine years.

As the children were growing up and needed less parental attention, Gillian, a very bright and accomplished woman, decided that she should "learn a trade." She had taught school in Britain but did not have the necessary qualifications in Canada to do that, and she did not want to do so anyway. She took a degree in social work and became particularly interested in group therapy. This led to work in an alcohol-counselling centre and then to an organization where she worked with various professionals to help mentally disabled people to function in the general population.

Gillian then began training as a psychotherapist and had some promising new career opportunities in Vancouver when Jonathan was offered a very attractive position at Syracuse University. This was a difficult decision for them because Jonathan's career was already flourishing at UBC, while Gillian's work as a psychotherapist was just beginning. The move would be of benefit to his career, but a setback for hers. Still, they both agreed that the Syracuse offer was too good to pass up and he accepted the position.

The move was indeed a good one for Jonathan's career as he went on to renown as one of the most distinguished of all contemporary philosophers. Gillian too was able, eventually, to pursue her work in Syracuse and developed a very successful private practice as a psychotherapist. They stayed in Syracuse for nineteen years.

In the late 1980s Gillian and Jonathan began to think ahead about where they might retire. They considered New Zealand, and Cambridge, and even Italy, but then realized that they would be unhappy being so far from their two children, both of whom were married with children and living in the Vancouver area.

Gillian made a trip back to Vancouver in 1989 and purchased a beautiful but overgrown rural property on Bowen Island, near Vancouver. They rented it out over the next eight years, always with the proviso that they could stay there for three weeks each summer, so they could try it out and see how they liked living there. They loved it and moved there permanently in 1997, after both retired. Jonathan spent much of the next seventeen years clearing brush from the property, better revealing the beautiful contours of the landscape there, as well as writing new, more accessible versions of many classical philosophical works and making them freely available on the internet. He was justifiably proud of both accomplishments, but I was unable to discern in which order.

Gillian and Jonathan spent seventeen happy years together on Bowen Island. When they moved there Jonathan was sixty-seven and Gillian a year younger. They very much enjoyed their quiet lives on the Island; they would sit for hours on a waterfront bench below their house, sometimes just silently enjoying the view, sometimes reminiscing and talking about their children and grandchildren, sometimes talking about their future. That future, they knew, was limited to relatively few years, but they were comfortable with that, happy with the lives they had been fortunate enough to lead.

For some years, though, Gillian was adamant about one thing: she did not want to live on beyond the point where she no longer was mentally competent. She did not want her body to be kept alive once her mind was gone.

And then her mind did start to leave her. In the few years before her death both she and Jonathan recognized that she was in the early stages of dementia. It began to get worse.

On that chosen day of August 18, 2014, Gillian and Jonathan climbed together, one last time, to a clifftop on their property, from where they could see their house and out across Collingwood Channel to Pasley Island and then beyond to Vancouver Island. After a short time they climbed back down to the base of the cliff where, the day before, Gillian had placed a mattress, wanting the cliffside as her final view. She lay down on the mattress and, at noon, took a lethal dose of Nembutal powder, a brand of pentobarbital used as a sedative but also, in higher amounts, for physician-assisted suicide in places such as Oregon where that is legal.

Gillian washed the Nembutal down with some water and then a swallow of scotch. Within three minutes she had peacefully fallen unconscious, and soon afterwards she was gone.

Earlier that day Gillian published her statement on a website called deadatnoon.com. It became widely quoted in media across the country, and is reproduced here in full:

> *August 18, 2014 — I will take my life today around noon. It is time. Dementia is taking its toll and I have nearly lost myself. I have nearly lost me. Jonathan, the straightest and brightest of men, will be at my side as a loving witness.*
>
> *I have known that I have dementia, a progressive loss of memory and judgment, for three years. It is a stealthy, stubborn and oh-so reliable disease. I might have preferred an exotic ailment whose name came trippingly off the tongue, but no, what I have is entirely typical. I find it a boring disease, and despite the sweetness and politeness of my family I am bright enough to be aware of how boring they find it, too. It is so rough on my husband, Jonathan. I don't think my lovely cat has noticed, but I'm not sure.*
>
> *Dementia gives no quarter and admits no bargaining. Research tells us that it's a "silent disease," one that can lurk for years or even decades before its symptoms become obvious. Ever so gradually at first, much faster now, I am turning into a vegetable. I find it hard to keep in my mind that my granddaughter is coming in three day's time and not today. "Where do we keep*

the X?" (coffee / milkshake-maker / backspace on my keyboard / the book I was just reading) happens all the time. I have constantly to monitor what I say in an attempt not to make some gross error of judgment.

There comes a time, in the progress of dementia, when one is no longer competent to guide one's own affairs. I want out before the day when I can no longer assess my situation, or take action to bring my life to an end. There could also come a time when I simply must make a decision based on my deteriorating physical health. I do not like hospitals — they are dirty places. Any doctor will tell you to stay out of them if you possibly can. I would not want a fall, a stroke, or some unforeseen complication to mess up my decision to cost Canada as little as possible in my declining years.

Understand that I am giving up nothing that I want by committing suicide. All I lose is an indefinite number of years of being a vegetable in a hospital setting, eating up the country's money but having not the faintest idea of who I am.

Each of us is born uniquely and dies uniquely. I think of dying as a final adventure with a predictably abrupt end. I know when it's time to leave and I do not find it scary.

There are so many things we obsess about. We seem to have a need to get things right. Should we bring a bottle of wine or some flowers to the party? Will jeans and my new boots work or is that too casual? How do I find a new mate?

We do NOT talk much about how we die.

Yet facing death is thoroughly interesting and absorbing and challenging. I have choices which I have reviewed, and either adopted or discarded. I think I have hit upon the right choice for me.

I have talked it over with friends and relatives. It is not a forbidden topic. Anything but.

Every day I lose bits of myself, and it's obvious that I am heading towards the state that all dementia patients eventually get to: not knowing who I am and requiring full-time care. I know as I write these words that within six months or nine months or twelve months, I, Gillian, will no longer be here. What is to be done with my carcass? It will be physically alive but there will be no one inside.

I have done my homework. I have reviewed my options:

1. Have a minder care for my mindless body. This would involve financial hardship for those I leave behind, or involve them in a seemingly endless round of chores that could erode even their fondest memories of me.

2. Request whatever care the government is willing to provide. (The facility will expect my husband, children, grandchildren, to visit often to thank the caretakers for how well they are looking after the carcass. Fair enough, but not what I wish for my family.)

3. End my own life by taking adequate barbiturates

to do the job before my mind has totally gone. Ethically, this seems to me the right thing to do.

I can live or vegetate for perhaps ten years in hospital at Canada's expense, costing anywhere from $50,000 to $75,000 per year. That is only the beginning of the damage. Nurses, who thought they were embarked on a career that had great meaning, find themselves perpetually changing my diapers and reporting on the physical changes of an empty husk. It is ludicrous, wasteful and unfair. My family, all of whom are rational and funny to boot, would not visit me in hospital, because they know I would not want them to.

The world strains under the weight of an aging population. We are living longer, and our life expectancies continue to grow. By 2045, the ratio of working-age citizens to their elderly dependents will become increasingly burdensome in almost every part of the world. In Canada and the US, the ratio is expected to be sixteen workers for every ten elderly dependents. It is a social and economic disaster in the making. Yet most people say they would like to live to 90 or 100, or even beyond.

There are many ethical issues here: life extension radically alters people's ideas of what it is to be human — and not for the better. As we, the elderly, undergo manifold operations and become gaga while taking up a hospital bed, our grandchildren's schooling, their educational, athletic, and cultural opportunities, will be squeezed dry.

The heart of the problem is arithmetic: The

post-World War ll Social Welfare State, created at a moment when the baby boom was still gestating, is built on a generational Ponzi scheme. As life expectancy increases and birth rates decline, the population pyramid is being inverted — and in some countries that is causing the entire economy to topple.

Everybody by the age of 50 who is mentally competent should make a Living Will that states how she wants to die, the circumstances under which she does not want to be resuscitated, etc. Add a statement such as: "If I am ill and frail and have an infection such as pneumonia, do not attempt to restore me to life with antibiotics. Pray let me pass. I do not give any relatives or doctors or psychiatrists the right to squelch this decision." One's general practitioner would have a copy.

Legally, everyone should have an obligation to make a Will, which would be stored electronically, could not be destroyed, and would be available automatically to any hospital in the world.

What about a person who refuses to make a Will? There should be a fallback Will that applies to everyone who has not done his civic duty. I do not have all the answers, but I do think I'm raising questions that need to be raised.

Three outsize institutions: the medical profession, the Law, and the Church will challenge and fight any transformative change. Yet we all hear of changes in each of these professions that suggest a broader approach, guided and informed by empathy. My hope is that all of these institutions will continue to transform themselves, and that the medical profession will mandate, through sensitive and appropriate protocols, the administration of a lethal dose to end the suffering of a terminally ill patient, in accordance with her Living Will.

Life seems somewhat like a party that I was dropped into. At first I was shy and awkward and didn't know what the rules were. I was afraid of doing the wrong thing. It turned out that I was there to enjoy myself and I didn't know how to do that. Someone kind talked to me and made me laugh. I began to understand that actually I had to make up my own rules and then live by them. I did pick up that I needed to know when to leave, and that is now.

All members of my immediate family are in Vancouver: daughter, son, two granddaughters and four grandsons. All know that it matters to me not to become a burden to them, or to Canada. I have discussed my situation with them all. In our family it is recognized that any adult has the right to make her own decision.

Just in case anyone is tempted to think I must be brave to off myself, you should know that I am a big sookie. I am sorely fearful of being alone in the dark. I am scared something will get me. I do not want to die alone. If my cat were failing in the way that I am, I would mix some sleeping medication in with top-quality ground beef, and when she fell asleep, carry her lovingly to the garden and do the rest. Who wants to die surrounded by strangers, no matter how excellent their care and competence?

I have had a husband beyond compare, and children and grandchildren who have outstripped me in most meaningful ways. Since I was seven I have had wonderful friends, whom I did and still do adore.

This is all much tougher than it need be on Jonathan, and I wish he did not have to be alone with his wife's corpse. Canadian law makes it a crime for anyone to assist a person committing suicide, and Jonathan, therefore, will in no way assist me. Our children, Sara and Guy, would so willingly be with their father, but the laws being what they are, we will not put them in jeopardy.

Today, now, I go cheerfully and so thankfully into that good night. Jonathan, the courageous, the faithful, the true and the gentle, surrounds me with company. I need no more.

It is almost noon.

* * *

And then she was gone. Jonathan, though he fully supported her decision, was stricken with grief. His voice cracked as he was interviewed for television. He knew what she did was the right thing to do, but he desperately missed his companion of almost sixty years. But he knew that he was losing her anyway, and he fully respected her wish not to descend into a vegetative state.

Gillian ended with "I need no more. It is almost noon." And surely we as Canadians needed no more to come to a humane decision on assisted death. It was almost time for the hearing by the Supreme Court of Canada. Gillian's words were widely circulated in the press and on the internet. Many hoped that the members of the Court would read them.

Calgary Herald *photograph of Dorothy and Victor Ramberg in December 11, 1941, after being found not guilty of murdering their son Christopher. The newspaper wrote, "When asked to allow their picture to be taken, Mr. Ramberg looked inquiringly at his wife, who smiled faintly: 'I don't see why not. Everyone has been so wonderful and kind to us both through all this'"* (Calgary Herald).

Sue Rodriguez with John Hofsess in September 1992, before the disagreement that split them apart (Lawrence McLagan).

Evelyn Martens in February 2005, a few months after her trial in November 2004 (Emrys Miller).

Dr. Donald Low walks through his laboratory in Toronto's Mt. Sinai Hospital February 19, 2008 (The Canadian Press/J.P. Moczulski).

Hollis Johnson and Lee Carter, lead plaintiffs in the B.C. Supreme Court case on assisted death (The Canadian Press/Fred Chartrand).

Gillian Bennett and her beloved cat, Coz 7 (Bennett family).

John Dixon, philosopher, author, human rights advocate and former President of B.C. Civil Liberties Association (John Dixon).

Robert Latimer answering questions from reporters at a news conference on his farm near Wilkie, Saskatchewan, in 1997 (The Canadian Press/Kevin Frayer).

CHAPTER 10
THE SUPREME COURT OF CANADA HEARING — 2014

The real question, of course, was what would the Supreme Court of Canada do with the B.C. Court's decision on assisted suicide? The hearing was on October 15, 2014.

To recap, on June 15, 2012, the B.C. Court ruling on the Carter et al. case, brought forward by the B.C. Civil Liberties Association, struck down the assisted suicide law, Section 241(b) of the *Criminal Code of Canada* (see Chapter 6). This landmark ruling by Justice Lynn Smith was thorough, powerful and decisive. Justice Smith showed how the law was in violation of the *Charter of Rights and Freedoms* and she instructed the federal legislature to rewrite the law within a year.

Smith's decision was appealed to the B.C. Court of Appeals by the Attorneys General of B.C. and of Canada. The appeal was heard by a panel of justices — B.C. Chief Justice Finch, and Justices Newbury and Saunders, who issued their ruling on October 10, 2013. The gist of it is covered by the final statement by Justices Newbury and Saunders:

> *In our respectful view, any review of the substantive* Charter *challenges, and the granting of comprehensive or limited relief from the effects of the law, are beyond the proper role of the court below and of this court. If the constitutional validity of s. 241 of the* Criminal Code *is to be reviewed notwithstanding* Rodriguez, *it is for the Supreme Court of Canada to do so. We would allow the appeal [and] set aside the trial judge's order. . .*

Because the 1993 Rodriguez case, similar to the 2012 Carter et al. case, had been adjudicated by the Supreme Court of Canada, the B.C. Court of Appeals determined that any changes to the precedent set in the earlier case should be made not by a lower court but by that same senior court.

This ruling of the B.C. Court of Appeals was disappointing, but probably did not make much difference. Had it supported Justice Smith's ruling, then the Attorneys General of B.C. and Canada would have appealed to the Canadian Supreme Court anyway. Final settlement of this controversial issue really needed to be sanctioned by the highest court of the country.

The Supreme Court of Canada did agree to rule on the case, and a public hearing was set.

The Supreme Court hearing was no small matter. An account by Simon Parcher of Ottawa, president of Canadian Humanist Publications (publishers of *Humanist Perspectives* magazine), gives a sense of the atmosphere:

It is a tranquil morning in Ottawa on Wednesday, October 15, 2014, with just enough rain falling to require the use of an umbrella. To the west of the Parliament Buildings, on a bluff high above the Ottawa River and set back from Wellington Street by an expanse of lawn, the Supreme Court of Canada Building dominates the landscape. On this day, its stately presence and majestic architecture will provide the setting for proceedings that will culminate in a momentous decision for all Canadians — one that is literally a matter of life and death.

The country's highest tribunal is about to hear oral arguments on the Carter vs. Canada *case. The outcome of this case will determine whether or not the law banning physician-assisted suicide in Canada violates the constitutional rights of Canadians. This decision will not only impact Canadians, but set an example as a landmark ruling that will influence court decisions all around the world.*

Several interest groups in support of striking down Canada's law that criminalizes physician-assisted suicide stood near the steps of the Supreme Court Building. A colorful display of umbrellas, placards and signage were in evidence as the demonstrators vied for the attention of onlookers and the media. Dying with Dignity Canada was perhaps the largest group present, with signs saying, "My Life. My Right. My Choice." and a large banner that read, "Why make people suffer when there is an alternative?" Individuals held up signs saying, "I'm a Canadian and I want a choice." and "Allow me to choose."

Further up on the Supreme Court steps, dozens lined up in the rain to get a public seat in the courtroom or to be part of the overflow crowd that watched the proceedings on closed circuit TV in the Grand Entrance Hall. Inside the doors there were another several dozen people waiting in an area that was cordoned off as security officials screened individuals before granting them further access. Members of the media with press passes were ushered past the waiting crowd.

The press had a visible presence in another cordoned-off section of the Grand Entrance Hall. An impressive display of large TV cameras panned the activity in the Hall and microphones resembling a long row of artillery were standing at attention, side-by-side, as several interviews took place simultaneously. It seemed that all the major media outlets from across the country were present. There was also a press table inside the courtroom where media types were set up with their laptops. This location provided an excellent vantage point from which reporters from publications like the Globe and Mail, *the* Toronto Star, *and myself from* Humanist Perspectives *magazine could observe and record the proceedings.*

Parcher commented on how circumstances have changed since the Rodriguez case:

Since then, the Netherlands, Belgium, Luxembourg

and some American states and the province of Quebec have passed laws allowing physician assisted suicide. In the interim, eight of the 1993 Canadian high court judges have retired. Only one of the original nine who deliberated the Rodriguez case, chief justice Beverley McLachlin, remains. She was one of the dissenting judges on that decision and found the law banning assisted suicide to be a Charter *violation.*

In the two decades since the Supreme Court denied Sue Rodriguez the right to doctor-assisted death, the issue has gained new prominence. Baby boomers and their parents are approaching the later chapters of their lives and polls are suggesting mounting support for assisted suicide.

Parcher went on to describe the room they had entered:

The Main Courtroom of the Supreme Court measures about forty feet by fifty feet and has black walnut walls between shallow rectangular columns. Six windows, three on each side of the room, rise from waist height up to the twenty-five-foot ceiling. In the center of the room are about thirty tables and red leather chairs for the legal counsel for the appellant, the respondent and the interveners (parties who have been added to the litigation). Along one side of the room is a long wooden desk with more red leather chairs for the press reporters. There is a similar set-up on the other side for the court reporters. At the back is bench seating to accommodate about eighty

observers. The courtroom is filled to capacity. The
nine justices enter the room, take their seats on
schedule at 9:00 a.m. and proceedings begin.

* * *

As he was for the B.C. Supreme Court case, Joe Arvay was
lead counsel for the plaintiffs. Arvay is described by John
Dixon of the B.C. Civil Liberties Association (BCCLA)
as being "widely recognized as the foremost constitutional
litigator in Canada, [having] argued several watershed civil
rights cases for the BCCLA." Now here he was in front of
the highest court, the court of final appeal, the court that
would decide, for many years into the future, how Canada
was going to deal with the matters of assisted suicide and
euthanasia. Whatever the Court decided this time would not
soon be revisited.

This Court decision would be it. And, to whatever extent
the justices had yet to make up their minds, it was squarely
up to Arvay to convince them to adopt a more progressive
position for the millions of Canadians who, if not actually
seeking assistance in dying themselves, would rest easier
knowing that such a thing as a gentle death could be made
possible.

If the Court upheld the Rodriguez decision of 1993, then
all of the efforts to change the law, over many years leading
up to this hearing, would be rendered futile.

If the earlier Court's decision was viewed as "good law,"
or even just as acceptable law, then the matter would not
likely be reopened any time soon.

What would the justices do? There was no way of knowing their views although we could guess that Chief Justice

McLachlin would be sympathetic. She had been so twenty-one years earlier in her minority opinion in the Rodriguez case. But the inclination of the others was not so clear. It was worrisome that six of the nine justices had been appointed by Conservative Party leader Stephen Harper. He was widely viewed as wanting to seek appointees who shared his socially conservative views. On the other hand, to Harper's apparent distress, the Court had proven not so compliant in recent years. Perhaps there was reason for hope that some of the compelling arguments in favour of allowing assisted suicide might this time prevail.

After preliminary comments, Arvay said:

> *This is a momentous occasion, for my clients, for society, for this court. This case quite simply concerns matters of life and death . . . the court [must] determine if the state has the right to require our family members, our friends, ourselves to endure intolerable suffering as a result of a medical condition when that suffering is worse than death itself.*

Arvay pointed out that Section 241(b) of the *Criminal Code of Canada* specifies a blanket prohibition of any sort of assisted death, and he stated that this criminalization of assistance in dying violates our *Charter of Rights and Freedoms*.

Arvay's argument was, in part, similar to the argument in the Rodriguez case. He repeated the argument about the law being discriminatory, according to Section 15 of the *Charter*: the law on assisted suicide means some disabled people are unable to take advantage of their right to commit suicide, a right that is available to able-bodied people.

However, the intervening twenty-one years had allowed

for the development of a much richer sense of Section 7 of the *Charter*, which protects the rights of life, liberty and security of the person. In documents presented to the court Arvay explained how Section 7 is violated by the law prohibiting assisted suicide. This argument was given in some detail, but to summarize:

- The right of life is lost when people in declining health decide they must end their lives prematurely, before they are so severely disabled that they will be unable to do it themselves.
- Liberty has to do with personal autonomy which should include the right to choose the time and manner of one's death.
- Security of the person concerns the right to bring an end to intolerable suffering.

As well as presenting his case that the law violated the *Charter*, Arvay needed to counter the expected arguments from the Attorneys General, that the issue of assisted death was a matter for the legislature to decide upon, not the courts: elected representatives of the people should decide about such a fundamental matter, not appointed judges. Arvay argued against this on two grounds. One was that judicial review by the Supreme Court was well established as the mechanism by which we decide if our laws are constitutional.

The second point Arvay made about this is that Parliament could revisit the issue, and pass laws that are compatible with the *Constitution*, but it was refusing to do so. The Prime Minister and the Solicitor General had repeatedly said they would not bring it forward. They justified this by stating that the matter has come before Parliament and has been defeated. Arvay pointed out, however, that it was raised only in private members' bills, which generally have little hope of success, and that even though there is strong public support for more progressive laws, political parties are very leery about tackling the issue because of the likelihood of alienating single-issue voters.

Arvay did not say this, but for clarification I should perhaps comment on how the political calculus works in this regard. Most voters support some version of assisted suicide and/or euthanasia, but they also have other issues they are concerned about, so supporting new end-of-life legislation will not guarantee their vote. Opponents of such legislation, on the other hand, often feel their opposition with a religious fervor that will override all other matters — their vote could well be determined by this one issue. For them it is a moral imperative, like their similar opposition to abortion, not just one of many political concerns. Introducing the matter in Parliament, then, in spite of its widespread popularity, might lose more votes than it gains. At least that is the fear of politicians, especially those on the right whose base of support is more likely to be overrepresented by opponents of new assisted-death legislation.

There was currently little hope that federal politicians would properly address this issue, and we were left with a law that violates our *Charter of Rights and Freedoms*. It is incumbent upon the Court, Arvay argued, to do something about this situation.

Arvay then asked the Court to imagine passing a law that made it a criminal matter for any physician to provide any sort of end-of-life care that might hasten death, such as withdrawing treatment that kept patients alive or applying palliative sedation that could shorten life. There would, Arvay said, be an outcry about this across the country, not least from the Canadian Medical Association, that has long endorsed such practices. But, Arvay argued, there are no "legal, ethical, moral or practical differences" between such a hypothetical law, which would be widely opposed, and the laws we currently have in regard to physician-assisted death in Canada.

The "vociferous" opposition to making physician-assisted death legally equivalent to those other accepted, morally equivalent practices comes, Arvay said, from some church groups and some organizations for the disabled.

"We respect your religious views," Arvay said, "but they cannot, in a secular society, trump our clients' constitutional rights."

Then, in a moment of great poignancy, Arvay, who has been confined to a wheelchair since an automobile accident earlier in his life, said, "I would be the very last person to ever suggest that one is 'better off dead' than being disabled." Arvay saluted the courage and determination of many disabled people in dealing with their physical impairments and leading dignified and rewarding lives.

However, it is wrong, Arvay argued, for some disabled people to determine what is an acceptable life for others. He also pointed out that the often-made argument that disabled people would be more vulnerable if physician-assisted death were permitted — that doctors would then be more inclined to end the lives of the disabled — was not supported by evidence from other jurisdictions.

The Attorneys General had, in documents presented to

the Court, introduced some "new evidence," the Montero affidavit, claiming that Belgium was on a slippery slope in regard to euthanasia, but this was another of the scare stories that inevitably appear and was handled convincingly by Arvay, just as earlier ones had been dealt with by Justice Smith at the B.C. Supreme Court ruling.

Much legal argument followed, with Arvay going over the fundamentals of the case for striking down the assisted suicide law, and going into legal details about how the existing law violates Section 7 and Section 15 of the *Charter*. He also made the case for why this matter, settled in the Rodriguez case, should be reopened. Arvay said that the Court's understanding of the meaning of Section 7 of the *Charter* had advanced since *Rodriguez*, and our understanding from other countries of the effectiveness of safeguards was now much more extensive than it had been in 1993. Toward the end of his comments, which were interspersed with many questions from the justices, the case was summed up by Justice Cromwell in this exchange:

> *JUSTICE CROMWELL. Mr. Arvay, do you*
> *accept that the centrepiece of the Rodriguez*
> *majority was the concern that nothing*
> *short of a blanket prohibition [as in 241(b)]*
> *would protect the vulnerable?*
> *ARVAY. Yes.*
> *JUSTICE CROMWELL. And your position,*
> *in a nutshell, is that you have established*
> *that that is not the case?*
> *ARVAY. Correct.*
> *JUSTICE CROMWELL. Thank you.*

This seemed a positive comment from Justice Cromwell who, as a Stephen Harper appointee, might have been expected to take a conservative position on assisted death. But there was no reason to assume so given his past record, where he had shown particular interests in teaching and in law reform. He was seen as firm but fair. As a Supreme Court judge, in 2014, he had headed up a report that recommended ways of improving access to justice in Canada. The report referred to trying to help with "problems of everyday people in everyday life." On this day, in this hearing in Ottawa, Arvay was talking about exactly such an issue.

Arvay's time was running out, but he sensed he should say a bit more about Justice Cromwell's comment; if the Court was going to see the issue about a blanket prohibition on assisted suicide and protection of the vulnerable as the crux of the matter, then he thought he should focus his final comments on that point. He quoted a remark that had been made by the Attorney General of Canada in regard to Justice Smith's B.C. Supreme Court ruling:

> . . . [Smith] was requiring Parliament to accept a level of risk with which she was comfortable, but which Parliament had specifically rejected.

The Attorney General had argued that Parliament, in passing Section 241(b) of the *Criminal Code*, had specifically indicated that, to prevent undue risk, nothing less than a blanket prohibition was necessary. Smith, he was saying, was wrong to challenge Parliament's view of acceptable risk.

But, Arvay argued, our understanding of risk has progressed to the point where it has become obvious that the blanket prohibition of assisted suicide has become a

Charter issue, and no longer can be defended by the claim of undue risk. If there is still some risk, he said, "Well, what level of risk is the Attorney General saying would be acceptable?" He pointed out that Smith had said that the risk can be "very substantially minimized." How much more can we expect than that? He talked about the impossibly high standard of zero risk, a standard that we do not meet anywhere in health care.

The lack of precision, however, seemed to worry Justice Moldaver. He spoke up asking for a clearer term than "very substantially minimized." Had Arvay given the Court a reason to doubt the safeguards, by being imprecise in defining the probability of error? Was Arvay sounding too cavalier about risk? Would the Court decide that any risk, especially undefined risk, is too much risk?

Arvay undoubtedly had carefully reviewed the backgrounds of the nine justices to help him understand the nature of any questions they might bring up and to help anticipate their concerns. Moldaver, Arvay would have known, was conservative but not, in the words of University of Ottawa law professor Adam Dodek, a "devout ideologue." He did, however, have a record of expressing his distaste for those who "clog the courts and tax an already overburdened justice system by bringing *Charter* and other applications that are baseless." So Arvay had to be careful here; Moldaver might see this case as a waste of time — as something that had already been settled in the Rodriguez ruling. And given his comment above, perhaps he agreed with the earlier Court's ruling in 1993 that the risk was too great, especially since it could not be clearly articulated.

Arvay pointed out that we accept risk in every aspect of life. There is some risk, he said, in ensuring any constitutional right. But here the safety of assisted suicide, in controlled circumstances, is "pretty close to beyond a reasonable doubt."

Justice Moldaver seemed satisfied and commented that "It's an acceptable risk," although it was unclear if he was stating his belief or just summarizing what Arvay had said. We would have to wait for the Court's final ruling to know if Moldaver, and indeed a majority of the other justices, would insist on no risk, and uphold the blanket prohibition of Section 241(b).

Finally, Arvay made a very important point about the costs of this constitutional challenge. Although Arvay did not mention his opponents in this regard, the representatives of the offices of the Attorneys General were receiving their regular paycheques for opposing this *Charter* challenge; Arvay and his colleagues were working pro bono. There was no big reward waiting for them when the matter was settled, as there might be in civil litigation. Why would lawyers be prepared to do this important constitutional work, and spend over a thousand of hours on it, as Arvay had, and not get paid? It is a flaw in the system that can only be rectified by having costs covered by court order.

The second speaker was Arvay's colleague, Sheila Tucker, who gave further details on a number of points that Arvay had raised, and made a particular effort to deal with a practice known as LAWER — Life-ending Action Without Explicit Request. This practice, which apparently is quite widespread in many countries, has been a concern for opponents of assisted suicide and euthanasia. They fear that the practice of LAWER is the beginning of a slippery-slope effect whereby the value of life will be downgraded and people will be callously disposed of for the sake of efficiency and convenience, and that passing a permissive law will exacerbate the risk.

LAWER is essentially non-voluntary hastening of death during the dying process. Usually it occurs with incompetent patients who are suffering greatly. Terminal sedation, when administered in such a way as to hasten death, would be one way this occurs.

There was some concern over LAWER when it came to public attention in the Netherlands in 1990, and opponents of assisted suicide in many countries used this concern as a reason to support their opposition. LAWER suggested, to some critics, that we need to tighten regulations about hastening death, not loosen them. This concern actually had an impact on the Rodriguez case, since it went along with the idea that a blanket prohibition of assisted suicide was necessary to prevent abuses.

The trouble with that argument is that the practice was actually going on even while the blanket prohibition was in place. Would it get worse with a more permissive policy? The evidence from the Netherlands and Belgium is that LAWER actually decreased when permissive legislation was passed; there was no slippery slope.

Studies have now shown that LAWER exists to a significant degree in many countries with absolute prohibitions of assisted suicide and euthanasia — countries such as Australia, Sweden and Italy. And it is clear now that permissive laws on assisted suicide and euthanasia do not lead to more unregulated assisted deaths.

Following Sheila Tucker there were interveners supporting the positions taken by her and by Arvay: the Government of Quebec, the Canadian Civil Liberties Association, the Alliance of People with Disabilities Who are Supportive of Legal Assisted Dying Society, Canadian Unitarian Council, and the Farewell Foundation for the Right to Die. The Canadian Medical Association also spoke, although it was not clear who or what it was supporting.

The support from the Alliance of People with Disabilities was striking and welcome. It has always seemed logical that disabled people should want to support permissive legislation on assisted suicide, as they are the ones discriminated against in the matter of suicide when they are deprived of that right because of physical handicaps. Their spokesperson, Angus Gunn, made two key points:

1. It is wrong to equate disability with vulnerability — people with disabilities are capable of making rational, voluntary and autonomous decisions to hasten their own deaths. As the law stands, vulnerability is uniformly imposed on an entire class of persons solely as a result of disability.

2. It is wrong to deprive "individuals of the quintessential expression of personal autonomy, namely how and when to die."

The Unitarian Council made a strong point about religious beliefs:

> *The faith groups on the other side . . . are no doubt sincere in their belief that physician-assisted death is fundamentally wrong, but coming from that same broad Christian faith tradition [we] reach exactly the opposite conclusion and we say that the Charter does not permit Parliament to prefer*

*what is merely one viable moral perspective over
another.*

Then, taking issue with Justice Sopinka, who wrote the
majority decision in the Rodriguez case:

*Every human life is of profound importance and
as individuals and as a society we should strive
to honour it but, respectfully, Justice Sopinka
was wrong in Rodriguez when he concluded that
active participation by one individual in the death
of another is "intrinsically morally and legally
wrong."*

The Canadian Medical Association said that they were
neither advocating nor speaking against physician-assisted
suicide, but merely putting forward cautions about how a
change in the law might affect physicians.

* * *

Speakers against changing the law began with Robert Frater,
representing the Attorney General of Canada.

"Chief Justice, Justices, our position is straightforward
here," said Frater. "*Rodriguez* is still good law."

There it was; there was the case that would decide what would
happen in the future to thousands, maybe millions, of dying
Canadians. Frater's position was that because this case had been
heard twenty-one years earlier — with far less relevant evidence
on hand, with much more legal interpretation of some clauses in
the *Charter*, with even then only five of nine judges supporting
the decision — that it was wrong to reopen the matter.

Frater went on to say:

> *The twin objectives of the legislation, protection of the vulnerable and the preservation of life, are as vital today as they were 21 years ago. There are no case law changes that mandate a departure from* Rodriguez, *there is no new legal consensus on any relevant issue in this country or abroad that mandates a change, there are no new facts that compel a reworking of the* Charter *analysis and there is no demonstration that this court's decision in* Rodriguez *is unworkable. The results should be the same.*

If this new case were to be lost, a majority of Supreme Court justices were going to have to buy the argument that there are no compelling new reasons to look at the law prohibiting assisted suicide. They would have to accept that understanding of the relevant issues had not progressed since 1993, and that there was no good reason to challenge the decision made then. The Court would have to accept the claim, among others, that there had been, "no demonstration that the court's decision in Rodriguez is unworkable."

Some observers undoubtedly thought that the suffering of terminally ill people across the country, some of whom every day pleaded to be released from their misery, only to be told by their doctors that "my hands are tied," had amply demonstrated that there were problems with the Rodriguez decision.

Perhaps trying to find some more solid ground to stand on, Frater turned to challenging the claims made by the representative from the Government of Quebec, who focused on the issue of jurisdiction (see Chapter 8), a matter not relevant to the central issue at hand at this hearing. Quebec was arguing that medically assisted death should be considered a medical matter and fall, therefore, under provincial jurisdiction. If that were to happen, however, it was going to emerge not from this session, but from some other one at some later date. At this hearing the issue was, to use Frater's description of it, to uphold the *Rodriguez* decision of twenty-one years ago, or not. But Frater used up three pages of testimony on the jurisdictional questions that were essentially irrelevant to this hearing and not even addressed by Arvay and the others.

Frater then tried an argument that seemed confused and that got him into trouble with at least one of the justices. He said that the decriminalization of attempted suicide, in 1972, was not an endorsement of suicide but an effort to find a better way of dealing with those who sought to die; something that in his view, apparently, is always wrong. Decriminalization of attempted suicide, then, was not really granting a right to suicide, Frater was claiming, but was seeking a way other than prosecution for treating those wishing to commit suicide. So, Frater argued, it is a misunderstanding of the purpose of the decriminalization to say that suicide is a right for the disabled.

But this was going nowhere. Decriminalization is decriminalization. Suicide is legal for everyone, and it should be so for everyone, not just the able-bodied. Justice Abella became quite agitated by Frater's argument and tackled him on it. She pointed out that however he wanted to describe the reasons for decriminalization of suicide, the law against assisted suicide was still discriminatory.

Abella was appointed by Liberal Prime Minister Paul Martin in 2004, and was well known for her interest in human rights. She could be counted on for a vote for liberalization of end-of-life laws. She seemed to have little patience with Frater, and with this particular argument that would come up again a little later in the proceedings.

Frater then switched to question the reasons Justice Smith had given for arguing that the Rodriguez decision should be challenged. For one thing, he claimed, her analysis of evidence from other jurisdictions was a task not for her but for legislators. She could present evidence from other jurisdictions but she should not, Frater argued, try to decide if the evidence was sufficient to negate legislation.

This odd view was immediately challenged by Justice Rothstein, who, in 2006, had been Stephen Harper's first appointment to the Court. He was known as being conservative but collegial. His question for Frater was a telling one:

But she was just looking at the evidence and that's what the evidence caused her to conclude. What's so legislative about that?

What indeed? If the Court is to decide on constitutionality of laws, as it is supposed to do, then surely it must make such judgments. Justice Abella added:

I would say it's not only not beyond her jurisdiction, she's answering the very question she's required to answer . . .

Perhaps unwisely, Frater continued on with this line of reasoning, prompting Justice Rothstein to jump back in:

But what are you arguing — what you are saying is that the trial judge is prohibited . . . I mean she had a mountain of evidence in front of her . . . She had to do something with it, she came to her conclusion. If the evidence was strong enough in her own opinion, I still don't get why she's not entitled to make the decision that she made . . .

Chief Justice McLachlin also found this argument of Frater's incomprehensible:

. . . having said 'we have to do this to protect the vulnerable,' you can't prevent the trial judge from examining that . . .

FRATER. Yes. No, no. I'm not saying she can't consider it at all, but the —

MCLACHLIN. I thought you did.

At this point the case being presented by the Attorney General of Canada was looking somewhat frayed. It did not get better for Frater as he continued trying to defend his position on Justice Smith who, McLachlin said, had looked at the evidence and said there are alternatives other than an absolute prohibition. "*Nothing wrong in her doing that, is there?*" McLachlin asked. Then Justices Abella, LeBel and Moldaver joined in the attack on Frater's position.

McLachlin, the Chief Justice, could be counted on to support more progressive legislation on assisted death. Lebel, as well, was expected to support a less restrictive law; he had been appointed by Liberal Jean Chrétien in 2000.

Eventually, after a lunch break, Frater shifted his position from saying that Justice Smith had no right to draw conclusions from the evidence from other countries to attacking the conclusions themselves, arguing that people had slipped through the Belgian system and the new "Montero" evidence was "disturbing." He also argued that the *Rodriguez* judgment making a blanket prohibition of assisted suicide and euthanasia had been confirmed by several developments since that judgment:

- High courts in the US, Ireland, the UK and the European Court of Human Rights have all subsequently rejected suicide and assisted suicide as a matter of constitutional right. So no legal consensus on the matter has emerged.
- A limited view of personal autonomy has emerged in Canadian law, not the broad view put forward by some that there is a right to suicide.
- Parliament has looked at evidence from foreign permissive schemes and voted repeatedly to maintain the blanket prohibition.
- There is not even a consensus in foreign permissive schemes — they are all different.
- There are particular cases, such as that of Alison Davis, a person with severe disabilities who says that if the law had been relaxed she would have ended her life, but, as it was not so, she went on to lead a fulfilling life. So vulnerable people like Alison Davis would be at risk.

But there were plenty of arguments that had contradicted

or would contradict these views. To summarize:

- There is no international legal consensus in favour of assisted suicide, but neither is there one against it.
- The limited view of personal autonomy put forward by Frater seems unjustified.
- Parliament has not looked seriously at, and seemingly will not look seriously at, the matter of assisted death, therefore leaving us with a law that is unconstitutional.
- The foreign progressive policies on the matter have some difference in details, as one would expect from complex legislative procedures, but they are all similar in general intent.
- The Davis case means nothing, because we do not know how serious she was about ending her life. It is an anecdote. Moreover, there was no application procedure at the time, and if there had been one of the kind Arvay was recommending, Davies would not likely have been accepted.

Frater yielded the floor to his colleague Ms. Nygard, who tackled the issue of Section 15 of the *Charter*, and the argument that severely disabled people are unable to have the same right to suicide as do able-bodied people. First she rejoined the argument Frater had unsuccessfully made in regard to the decriminalization of suicide. She repeated the view that the purpose of that decriminalization was not to grant the right of suicide but to find better ways of preventing and dissuading people from committing suicide. This is an important factor, according to Nygard, "in looking at whether the prohibition against assisted suicide is discriminatory."

But is it an important factor? Justice Abella did not seem to think so. She questioned Nygard, as she had questioned Frater, asking "do you accept that it has a disparate impact on persons with disabilities?" Nygard agreed it did, but seemed to think that would be insufficient to render the law unconstitutional. She explained her view:

> . . . *that societal reality* [for people with disabilities] *is one in which there is exists a prevalent bias, including within the medical profession, which devalues the lives of individuals with disabilities . . . doctors consistently perceive the quality of the lives of their patient with disabilities to be significantly lower than those patients themselves experience their lives . . . sometimes able-bodied, independent and privileged medical professionals can't even imagine that a life which is lived with physical restrictions in which there is dependence on others for care can also be nonetheless a meaningful, productive and fulfilling life.*

As a result of this bias, Nygard claimed, "a request for hastened death from an individual with a disability is responded to in a very different manner than that same request from an able-bodied person."

Justice Abella pointed out that this was an argument that the disabled need protection against their own wishes, a perception that was shared by Chief Justice McLachlin.

MCLACHLIN. There is something stereo-
typical about your argument that's kind
of bothering me. In other words, "they,"
"all of them," need protection, a leg up, a
different treatment.
NYGARD. No.

Nygard was in trouble here because she had decided to try
to show that there is no Section 15 violation of the *Charter*
because the disabled are discriminated against by society in
general and in that context they will be treated badly if it
comes to requesting suicide — not that they will be denied,
but that they will too readily be accepted. But the evidence
from other countries contradicts this idea, as Justice Smith
had shown. Furthermore, the idea that the disabled had to
be protected from their own wishes seemed patronizing.

The Frater/Nygard team was not faring well. It did not
get any better. After some further comments by Nygard this
exchange occurred:

JUSTICE CROMWELL. Could I just ask
you a couple of things? Do you accept that
one of the effects of the law [Section 241(b)]
is to prolong suffering?
NYGARD. One of the effects of the law can be
to prolong suffering, yes.
CROMWELL. Well. Not "can be."
NYGARD. In some circumstances will be,
yes.
CROMWELL. And do you accept as well the
proposition that another effect of the law is
to have people kill themselves prematurely?

NYGARD. I don't know that that can fairly
be said to be an effect of the law.
CROMWELL. There was a finding of fact to
that effect.
NYGARD. You may be right about that.
CROMWELL. Do you accept that finding or
are you challenging it?
NYGARD. No, I won't be challenging it.
CROMWELL. So where does that impact get
taken into account in the context you have
been telling us about?
NYGARD. Those impacts can't be ignored,
but the entire —
CROMWELL. I think your side of the room
has been ignoring them, that's why I'm
asking where they fit in the analysis.
NYGARD. No. That's why I say these are
very difficult issues. There is no easy
answer here . . .

She went on at some length, speaking of "these percep-
tions of the lower quality of life led by people with disabilities
they don't themselves experience."

CROMWELL. I gave you two examples of
other messages that [your position] sends,
that your suffering doesn't matter and
the fact that you may kill yourself sooner
doesn't matter . . . and you say those
matters shouldn't be ignored?
NYGARD. No, they shouldn't.
CROMWELL. But where in your analysis do

they get taken into account?

Nygard had no real answer to this question.

Next was the representative of the Attorney General of Ontario, who questioned the legitimacy of Justice Smith's ruling on the grounds that it violated a Supreme Court precedent, but did not add anything of value to the fundamental discussion about the law being unconstitutional.

The case against Justice Smith and her B.C. Supreme Court ruling did not seem to be faring well, at least by my reckoning, nor was it made more convincing by the next speaker, Bryant Mackey, representing the Attorney General of British Columbia. Mackey started by taking issue with Joe Arvay's plea for legal costs to be covered by government. Mackey, who himself was undoubtedly receiving a substantial salary for his work representing an office of the B.C. Government, mentioned "respect for the public purse" in wanting to deny costs for Arvay; he did not mention the possibility of foregoing his own salary out of respect for that purse. He worried that approving costs might become the norm in constitutional cases, rather than the exception.

In response to this Justice LeBel asked, "Well, I would perhaps ask you, if this case is not important enough for special costs, what kind of case will really make the cut?"

Mackey continued to argue his case to deny funding. Why, I wondered, were the Attorneys General so adamant about trying to deny funding for this case. The reason, I was advised by a knowledgeable observer, is that Attorneys General see their role as enforcing and upholding the law, and they have little interest in the matter of constitutional challenges, which throw existing laws into question. Their most effective way of discouraging such challenges is to cut off funding for them, hence the expressed fear by Mr. Mackey that public funding of constitutional challenges might become the "norm." That would be, for him, a nightmare.

Denying of funding for Arvay and his team was the only issue pursued by the representative of the B.C. Attorney General. Funding for constitutional challenges, if not granted by the Court, does often materialize in some form from charitable or other organizations, but it is haphazard, minimal and not guaranteed.

Next up was David Baker, representing the Council of Canadians with Disabilities. His arguments were familiar ones:

- The law, 241(b), is a "necessary protection for all Canadians."
- People with disabilities need the protection of the law as much as or more than their non-disabled peers.
- Changing the law will only add to the feelings of despair felt by persons with disabilities.
- Relaxation of the law would undermine the protection of life and lead to abuses.

None of these points seemed to impress the justices, and they had been mostly addressed by Arvay.

Following Baker was Geoffray Trotter, representing the Evangelical Fellowship of Canada. His argument was about the sanctity of life and then he made this strange point:

Why should our tolerance for the death of the

innocent be any higher when those at risk are the
disabled rather than the convicted?

Trotter's point, I guess, is that as we do not allow capital punishment for murderers, why should we be so cavalier about killing those innocent of any crime? This is not the most acute of arguments. Supporting assisted death has nothing to do with punishing people; it is about granting mercy to those who desperately seek to die.

Trotter talked of the *Charter*'s commitment to the "inherent worth and dignity of every individual," taking it to mean that "no Canadian is better off dead than alive." But surely the *Charter* does not have such a narrow intent. The worth and dignity of an individual can be confirmed, not denied, by the provision of a humane exit from a life that is felt by the person living it to have become worse than death.

Justice Cromwell probed one of the central weaknesses that lurks behind the arguments of many evangelicals:

> CROMWELL. *Would it follow from your*
> *submissions [regarding the sanctity of life]*
> *that capital punishment would never be*
> *constitutionally permitted?*
> TROTTER. *I'm not sure, Justice Cromwell,*
> *but I do know that the death of one innocent*
> *person is one too many . . .*
> CROMWELL. *But you seem to be submitting*
> *a very absolutist proposition of the sanctity*
> *of life and I just wondered if in your analy-*
> *sis it has any limits.*

Trotter avoided the thrust of the question, because, if not he himself, then many of his clients famously support capital punishment. I guess his defence here, which he seemed to want to obfuscate, was that capital punishment involved the death of those who were not "innocent." So sanctity of life apparently refers only to innocent life, which of course makes the concept all the more problematic.

Next were presentations by representatives of the Collectif des Médicins Contre L'Euthanasie and then the Catholic Civil Rights League. The latter argued that its position was independent of its religious beliefs, but it is opposed to there being a legal duty for doctors to kill patients and doctors whose are opposed to assisted death should not have to refer patients to someone who will do the deed. This argument, not germane to the central issues at hand, did not seem to have much traction with the justices.

Joe Arvay was given a brief amount of time to respond. He questioned a suggestion made by the Canadian Medical Association that Justice Smith's views, about doctors' ability to assessing the competency of patients, lacked a "real-world" perspective. In other words, she lacked the understanding of the issues that a genuine doctor would have. In fact, Arvay said, her comments were based upon the testimony of real-world doctors, many of whom were members of the CMA. He also questioned the CMA's fears that if the law were struck down there would be no ongoing consultation with doctors in regard to how we should proceed. Of course there would be such consultation. Then Arvay challenged Frater's claim that Justice Smith made errors of fact when ruling that safeguards could eliminate most risk. In fact her view came from careful examination of a lot of evidence.

Arvay tackled Frater on his "grossly overstated" problems of compliance with regulations, in foreign jurisdictions with permissive laws. Justice Smith, in her detailed examination of all of the evidence, had found no serious violations of regulations.

Arvay also challenged references Frater and others made to palliative sedation as a means of handling serious suffering at the end of life. Of palliative sedation Arvay said:

> *It's when a doctor injects a barbiturate into a patient and puts that patient into a deep and continuous coma and then usually withdraws any kind of nutrition or hydration . . . there are no guidelines about it, there is no law about it . . . it can be either too little or too late . . . the only time [most doctors] will ever allow palliative sedation is in the last hours or days of the dying process . . . it's hardly an answer to what we need for people who, like Gloria Taylor and Sue Rodriguez, see the end coming but it's still many months away, many months of suffering.*

He mentioned that there apparently are some doctors who practice palliative sedation maybe weeks or even months before death is expected. And with no hydration or feeding, as is often the case, death will be much hastened. How is that different, Arvay asked, from physician-assisted dying? So either palliative sedation comes right at the end of life, which is too late for some, or it comes earlier and is the same thing as physician-assisted dying.

Arvay also challenged the notion that the disabled do have access to suicide: they can just starve themselves. But this is a very painful, prolonged, awful death. He said starvation is not even on the list from Stats Canada of the ways people kill themselves. "It's a horrific way of dying," Arvay said.

It is true, Arvay allowed, as Baker had argued earlier, that sometimes people's wish to die is "transitory and situational," which is why new legislation should recommend assessment of the patient's mental state, and reasonably lengthy waiting periods.

Finally, Arvay discussed the views of Ms. Nygard, who said that doctors perceive the value of lives of the disabled as less than that of able-bodied people, suggesting that doctors would be more likely to assist in the death of disabled people. But the evidence, brought out in the B.C. Supreme Court case, had been just the opposite. Then he added:

> *But, you know what, it doesn't matter. The only thing that matters is that the doctor has to ask the disabled person, 'Do you want to live or do you not want to live?' and then have a searching inquiry of that and respect the disabled person's decision like we would anybody else's decision.*

With that the proceedings closed.

To my eyes and ears Arvay and his supporters had pummeled the opposition on this day of the Supreme Court of Canada hearing. Surely they had won the day. Or had they?

They had.

CHAPTER 11
THE HISTORIC DECISION — 2015

The ruling appeared on February 6, 2015. It was a historic vindication of Justice Smith and of the opinions of the many people who have felt that Section 241(b) of the *Criminal Code of Canada* was an affront to personal autonomy and prevented merciful treatment of severely ill people.

"The appeal should be allowed," reads the opening line of the unanimous Court decision — referring to the appeal by Arvay and the original plaintiffs to sustain the original ruling by Smith. (The full ruling is given in Appendix 5.) The decision entailed striking down Section 241(b), the prohibition of assisted suicide, as well as the related Section 14:

Section 241(b) reads:

> *Everyone who aids or abets a person to commit suicide, whether suicide ensues or not, is guilty of*

*an indictable offence and is liable to imprisonment
for a term not exceeding fourteen years.*

Section 14:

*No person is entitled to consent to have death
inflicted on him, and such consent does not affect
the criminal responsibility of any person by whom
death may be inflicted on the person by whom
consent is given.*

The Court's ruling specified that physician-assisted death
should be allowed for:

*competent adult persons who (1) clearly consent
to the termination of life and (2) have a grievous
and irremediable medical condition (including an
illness, disease or disability) that causes enduring
suffering that is intolerable to the individual in the
circumstances of his or her condition.*

The Court used the term "physician-assisted death,"
rather than "physician-assisted suicide," leaving it for the
legislators to determine what exactly will be allowed. Since
it is 241(b), the prohibition of assisted suicide, that was
being declared unconstitutional, then new legislation must
(one assumes) at least provide for the legalization of assisted
suicide. But because the Court speaks of assisted death,
rather than assisted suicide, it appears to leave an opening, although not a requirement, for voluntary euthanasia
as well: legislation could allow the final step to be taken by
someone else. Assisted suicide is allowed in Switzerland and

some US states. Voluntary euthanasia is allowed in Belgium and the Netherlands.

The decision of the Court was based upon the determination that the existing laws were a violation of Section 7 of the *Charter*. The Court wrote:

> *Insofar as they prohibit physician-assisted dying for competent adults who seek such assistance as a result of a grievous and irremediable medical condition that causes enduring and intolerable suffering, ss. 241 (b) and 14 of the* Criminal Code *deprive these adults of their right to life, liberty and security of the person under s. 7 of the* Charter .

Interestingly, this decision of the Court was based solely on Section 7 of the *Charter*, which guarantees the right "life, liberty and security of the person." Life, the Court argued, is jeopardized when certain individuals are forced to end their lives prematurely, while they are still able, themselves, to do so. "Liberty and security of the person," to the Court, was also relevant to their judgment because,

> *An individual's response to a grievous and irremediable medical condition is a matter critical to their dignity and autonomy. The prohibition denies people in this situation the right to make decisions concerning their bodily integrity and medical care and thus trenches on their liberty. And by leaving them to endure intolerable suffering, it impinges on their security of the person.*

The Court did not rule on Section 15 of the *Charter*, concerning discrimination against the disabled (that some disabled people were unable to avail themselves of the rights others have to commit suicide). This had been brought up as another area of possible violation of the *Charter*, but because the Court had already ruled that the law against assisted suicide violated Section 7, it was unnecessary to rule on Section 15. The striking down of the laws was put on hold for twelve months to allow time for legislators to formulate new laws to replace them.

The Court also ordered that the entire costs for bringing this case forward to the courts, from the beginning at the B.C. Supreme Court to the Supreme Court of Canada, would be covered by the Government of Canada (90%) and the Attorney General of B.C. (10%). This was due in part to the Court's statement that the case "involved matters of public interest that are truly exceptional," and "that they have a significant and widespread societal impact."

The awarding of costs here is exceedingly important for at least two reasons. One is the matter of fairness in having both sides in such disputes on matters of public interest, not just the government employees, be compensated with public money. The second reason is that the legal pursuit of *Charter* challenges is not a lucrative one at the best of times, and getting lawyers like Joe Arvay is essential to winning these cases. Such lawyers will still put themselves at a financial disadvantage in taking on such cases, as opposed, say, to civil cases with big payoffs, but they will be more likely to join fundamental constitutional battles that will determine what sort of country we are going to have, if they can be confident that at least basic costs will be covered.

The victory at the Court, on February 6, 2015, was clear,

decisive and remarkable for its unanimity. This was, after all, a Court that, insofar as he was able to do it, had been stacked by Conservative Prime Minister Stephen Harper. Harper, a social conservative, with his main base of support in Canada similarly oriented, may have considered somehow challenging the Court's decision. Perhaps if the vote had been close he could have launched an attack on the "liberal" members of the Court and asserted that McLachlin, as a carryover from earlier days did not reflect the current will of the people. A close vote would have given government more reason to quibble and perhaps stall. But the 9-0 decision made any opposition problematic.

* * *

Following the announcement of the Supreme Court's ruling, the B.C. Civil Liberties Association, which had orchestrated and sustained this entire constitutional challenge, issued an immediate press release:

> *Today is a historic day for Canadians. This morning, the Supreme Court of Canada issued its unanimous decision in the BCCLA's dying with dignity case,* Carter v. Canada, *striking down the criminal ban on physician assisted dying. The Court recognized that seriously and incurably ill Canadians have the fundamental right to make their own decisions about end of life care.*
>
> *Today, decades of work by so many Canadians has finally achieved this important victory for compassion and autonomy for those who suffer from serious and irremediable medical conditions,*

whether an illness, a disease or a disability.
The BCCLA and the families behind this case
are overjoyed . . .

CEO Wanda Morris of Dying with Dignity Canada said:

We're deeply heartened by the court's compassion towards those who suffer unbearably or face the prospect of a horrific death. This is a fantastic victory, and today we rejoice with the 84 per cent of Canadians who support the right to compassion and choice at end of life.

Striking down the ban on assisted dying is a crucial step towards a future in which all Canadians are afforded the right to die with dignity.

In our work, we field hundreds of calls every year from individuals who face the prospect of great suffering. How wonderful is it that they may soon face that prospect with equanimity. They will know that, if worst comes to the worst, our medical system will not abandon them, but rather offer them choice.

The occasion is also bittersweet because of the scale of tragedy and loss advocates for end-of-life choice have endured along the way. My thoughts turn to people for whom the decision came too late, men and women with conditions like Huntington's Disease and ALS who ended their lives violently and prematurely because they feared their final wishes wouldn't be carried out.

The Euthanasia Prevention Coalition was not so happy. Its press release stated that, "the Supreme Court of Canada has decided not to protect people from assisted suicide . . . an activist decision."

An Unsolved Problem

The Supreme Court decision still does nothing for children like Christopher Ramberg and Tracy Latimer. Their cases helped build public sympathy for assisted death, but no way has been found to help children like them. Such children will be left to suffer an existence of relentless pain, unless their parents will do what Dorothy Ramberg said she and her husband decided to do about their son and his terrible situation.

Those parents who make that merciful decision will then, if they are caught, be charged with murder and prosecuted; and, given the Latimer precedent, will probably be found guilty. Children like Christopher Ramberg and Tracy Latimer will be left to suffer, unless their parents are willing to risk their freedom to save their children from further suffering.

Still, Canada has, with its Supreme Court ruling striking down the prohibition of assisted suicide, taken a major step toward rational and fair treatment of the terminally afflicted. In the future, a man like Allan Scott (see the Introduction) will be able to choose for himself as humane a death as he granted his pet. This does not solve all end-of-life problems, but at least it was a very good start.

* * *

One more important point should be emphasized. In the heat of battle it is easy to dismiss, too lightly, the concerns of the opposition. But there is a need to think clearly and carefully about those concerns. The Euthanasia Prevention Coalition and other Canadians have both religious and practical concerns about assisted death. In responding to the Court's decision the Coalition wrote:

> *Giving doctors the right to cause the death of their patients will never be safe and no amount of "so-called safeguards" will protect those who live with depression or abuse. There will always be people who will abuse the power to cause death and there will always be more reasons to cause death . . . Assisted suicide creates new paths of abuse of elders, people with disabilities and other socially deprived people. The scourge of elder abuse in our culture continues to grow . . . Assisted suicide is an abandonment of people who live with depression who require support and proper care.*

These are real concerns that need to be considered seriously and thoughtfully.

In Chapter 1, I quoted John Dixon and the life-changing experience he had with a dying friend, and how this had influenced him in his later battles to get the laws on assisted death changed. He was instrumental in getting the B.C. Civil Liberties Association to lead the successful B.C. Supreme Court challenge of the law. I asked Dixon about his thoughts on the Supreme Court decision and the historic victory for the cause for which he had fought for so long. His response was to urge caution in victory:

As I expect is the case with most persons turning to this book, I'm delighted with the decision of the Supreme Court in Carter v. Canada. *In fact, I prepared and swore the affidavit of the B.C. Civil Liberties Association in its role as co-petitioner with Carter. I was president of the BCCLA when the case was conceived.*

I am also pro-choice, and was in the forefront of the opposition to the attempt by the B.C. Government, in 1988, to cut medicare funding for any and all abortions. In fact, I assisted in the preparation of the successful Civil Liberties case against the government with Phil Bryden and J. J. Camp.

So I'm a small "l" liberal, and clearly not averse to using the legal system to advance civil libertarian positions on the beginning and end of life issues.

but . . . and I want to be careful to keep that "b" in lower case, I would like to use this opportunity to at least whisper some reservations about liberalizing enthusiasm, and the importance of respecting those who disagree with us. Fighting for a cause — especially effective fighting — requires the enlistment of emotional energy if you are going to stay the course and prevail. So there is abundant animus on opposing sides of deeply divisive issues such as abortion and euthanasia: a considerable amount of noise competing with dispassionate deliberation. Which extends, if we dare whisper it, to the very dignified and formalized combat in our courts of law, and even our universities.

Justice Learned Hand, who is generally — and I think correctly — regarded as one of the wisest liberal judges to sit on an American high court, offered this advice: "The spirit of liberty is the spirit which is not too sure that it is right."

From a very different perspective — a very conservative one — we have Edmund Burke's defence of respect for what he called "just prejudice". Burke cautioned against enthusiasm for discarding long-standing societal prejudices. Anticipating Darwin, he suggested that we approach taboos as the product of a cultural evolutionary process that produces strong, negative, emotional response to behaviour that threatens the survival of societies that permit indulgence in them.

Against those of us who have fought for the Supreme Court decision in Carter, *are those who revere the taboo against the taking of innocent human life — whether the lives be of the unborn, or sick and dying. They have heard our plea for intelligence over habit, thought over emotion, and liberalizing policies over ancient prejudice, and they are unmoved. As Justice Sopinka was unmoved in* Rodriguez — *the legal preface to* Carter — *in his appeal to the "sanctity of life" he saw as protected in the Charter right to life, liberty, and security of the person.*

I thought that appeal was perverse — a twisted reading of section seven of the Charter that went against the secular spirit of our constitution. I much preferred the wisdom of Chief Justice McEachern of the B.C. Supreme Court who commented, in his reasons for the dissent in Rodriguez, *as decided by his court, that "death is part of life." That perspective was echoed by Justice Peter Cory when* Rodriguez *was heard at the Supreme Court of Canada, resulting in the narrowest 5 to 4 majority against the pleadings of Sue Rodriguez. I thought, and declared at the time, that that decision was a terrible misfortune — a missed opportunity.*

But still . . . in the spirit of Learned Hand and Burke, it behooves us innovators to give honest consideration to the possible wisdom — whole or partial — of our opponents.

Ancient Jewish law — you can look it up, as Yogi Berra said — took a very serious view of the quality of judgment when a human life was on the line. So seriously, that if a jury in a capital case brought in a unanimous guilty verdict, the accused was acquitted. The reasoning was that if there was unanimity, the deliberations must have been superficial! Further, and for good measure, the jurists of the religious court — a Beth Din *— who found the accused guilty, had to personally carry out the execution. Since one of the methods of execution was pouring molten lead down the throat of the condemned, that provision may have discouraged a rush to judgment.*

Hard to resist an affectionate response to that lovely, ironic, wry Jewish wisdom. Maimonides, the great twelfth-century Jewish intellectual and jurist, famously preferred that a thousand guilty persons were acquitted than one innocent one should be wrongly convicted and killed. There is a metric there that underscores the abhorrence of taking innocent life, however carefully the decision to kill is taken.

In the year provided by the Supreme Court for the government to provide the legislative rubber on the road to a functioning framework for physician assisted suicide, there will be a lot of hard work for everyone concerned. It would be remarkable if there weren't a struggle at every level and stage of the process, given the strength of the convictions and commitment of those involved.

Professor Joseph Tussman of the University of California at Berkeley (student of Alexander Meiklejohn, who was a long term member of the National Committee of the American Civil Liberties Union) once suggested to me — at least half seriously — a way of guarding the integrity of debate over issues as contentious as those concerned with the beginning and end of human life. "Every person who aspires to address these issues in the public space should be required to first provide a most concise and persuasive case for the side they oppose. If they fail in this effort, or refuse to participate in it, they should not be accorded the freedom of the forum. They have shown they have nothing to contribute beyond war cries."

Not going to happen of course, but it at least suggests a model of procedure that Learned Hand and Burke might approve. We liberalizers have had our legal prayer answered, and we should be mindful of how dangerous that can be. A year (a significant part of which is already gone) is not a long time when so much must be accomplished, and sober, sensitive, considerate voices will be at a premium.

* * *

Now it was time for sober, sensitive and considerate voices to find a way to respect the concerns of those fearful about the Court's decision, but at the same time respond to the legacy for reform articulated in that decision.

CHAPTER 12
RESPONDING TO UNJUST LAWS

"There is a higher court than courts of justice and that is the court of conscience. It supersedes all other courts."
— Mohandas Gandhi

A fundamental question raised by this book is: What should we do about laws we perceive to be unjust?

These stories illustrate various ways people have tried to circumvent what they saw as unjust laws prohibiting assisted suicide and euthanasia. The Rambergs and Robert Latimer simply could see no choice but to break the law — there was no other way to prevent their children from suffering. The Rambergs risked their lives in doing this; Latimer sacrificed many years of his. In many of the other stories recounted here, the justice system, including juries, prosecutors and judges, has refused to prosecute acts of mercy — technically, crimes — to the full extent possible under the law. John Hofsess and Evelyn Martens went underground to help desperate people who wanted to die. Sue Rodriguez openly petitioned the courts to change the law to permit assistance in dying, and then two decades later the B.C. Civil Liberties Association and other plaintiffs did the same thing, this time successfully. But all of the stories recounted here highlight some version of personal struggles involving conscience coming into conflict with the law.

Should we not fully respect the law, even when a particular one seems wrong? The case for the law being sacrosanct is not a trivial one. If not the law, then who decides what is right? Do we not want rule of law rather than rule of individuals? If we let everyone decide for himself or herself what is right, then we run into the problem of self-deception: when it is in our interests to do so we can fool ourselves into thinking that an illegal action is right. Moreover, there are sociopaths who do not even need to fool themselves about this — they do not care whether or not their actions are either legal or right. So we need laws, not individuals, to determine what we are allowed to do.

Are we obliged, then, from an ethical standpoint, to follow the law in all circumstances? Do our ethical obligations — our responsibility to do the right thing — begin and end with the law?

Henry Morgentaler, when he was being prosecuted for carrying out illegal abortions, asked the following question: If you saw a person drowning in a pond, but there was a sign prohibiting access to the pond, would you trespass to save the person?

So what about that drowning person? What about the thousands of women illegally saved, by Henry Morgentaler, from bearing unwanted children, or from suffering injury or death at the hands of back-alley abortionists? It is easy simply to dismiss individual conscience and insist on following the law. But if we deeply believe that following a particular law is wrong, especially when the well-being of others is at stake, then it is hard to escape the conclusion that our ethical obligation is to go against that law.

* * *

These are not easy issues, and we should be troubled by them. As I was working on this book I happened to visit Eike-Henner Kluge, the philosopher at the University of Victoria who is one of Canada's foremost bioethicists. He was involved in the Rodriguez case and was the founding Director of the Department of Ethical and Legal Affairs for the Canadian Medical Association. He has written extensively and influentially about end-of-life matters. Over the years I have been much impressed with Kluge's involvement in practical, real-life problems (unlike a great many of his philosophical colleagues). I thought that if anyone could give me help with this ethical problem it was he.

When we met he emphasized that, while he had worked hard over the years in support of a more progressive assisted-death law, the possible abuses that concern many people must not be ignored.

"First we must understand that the limitations of the law, including the assisted-suicide law, are not based on trivial or foolish concerns," he said. "If we do change the law we must be keenly aware of the possibilities of abuse, and we must be very careful to have adequate safeguards."

He went on to talk about how close to home some

unethical practices have been in the past. At the Canadian Medical Association, he had encountered some doctors who had been involved in some highly questionable activities. One was a doctor who had been implicated in one of the most infamous medical experiments in the history of the United States — the Willowbrook Experiment. The Willowbrook State School, in Staten Island, New York, was an institution for intellectually disabled children that opened in 1947 and closed in 1987. New York senator Robert Kennedy called the institution a "snake pit," and noted that the overcrowded facility had people living in "filth and dirt." The worst part, though, was the medical experimentation on children there, particularly one involving experimental treatment of hepatitis. The experiment included infecting children with hepatitis by injecting them with the virus, or by feeding them milkshakes infused with feces from other infected children.

Another doctor encountered by Eike-Henner had participated in perhaps the most unethical medical experiment in Canadian history — the brainwashing experiments, funded by the CIA, that were carried out at the Allan Memorial Institute at McGill University in Montreal, from 1957 to 1964. These experiments were carried out under the direction of Dr. Ewen Cameron. Without the opportunity for informed consent, patients were subjected to attempts to "break down ongoing patterns of patients' behaviour by particularly intensive electroshocks," called "depatterning," and "intensive repetition (16 hours a day for 6-7 days) of a prearranged verbal signal." Some patients were put to sleep for seven to ten days at a time and some were given LSD — "treatments" that were applied to the uninformed, unknowing patients at the Institute.

These horrors perpetrated so close to home illustrate,

for Eike-Henner, the reason for the extreme concern expressed by some opponents of assisted suicide and euthanasia, concerns that we ought not lightly to dismiss. If we open the door to any such practices, could we be opening it to the egregious sort of abuse of patients that occurred in Willowbrook and at the Allan Memorial Institute? The opponents of the sort of legal change that is argued for in this book — legalization of physician-assisted suicide and euthanasia — point to how easily, it seems, such things can happen, even at the hands of eminent doctors and caregivers. They happened in Nazi Germany, to be sure; but they happened here, too.

I asked Eike-Henner if he thought the risk of such things was too great if we legalized assisted death. He referred me to his arguments on this same point that appear in his recent book *Ethics in Health Care: A Canadian Focus*. In his book Eike-Henner quotes David Hume:

> *There is no method of reasoning more common, and yet more blamable than . . . to endeavor to refute any hypothesis by pretext of its dangerous consequences.*

It is true, Eike-Henner pointed out, that bad things can ensue from many, perhaps all, types of legislation. All of criminal law, in fact, runs the considerable risk of punishing innocent people. What must happen is not to prohibit potentially problematic legislation, if it is fundamentally sound and good for the people of the country, and wanted by them, but to establish such legislation with appropriate safeguards against abuses. Eike-Henner points to legislation in other countries that has achieved this.

I wondered if the doctor who had worked with Cameron had any regrets about what he had done at the Institute. "None at all," Eike-Henner said. "He said he was just a resident there. He said none of it was his responsibility — he just went along with what they were doing. He felt that he did no wrong."

I asked how Eike-Henner came by his own moral firmness — what motivated him to be the way he is.

"There were two people who deeply influenced me," he said. "One was Albert Schweitzer, who used a phrase that struck me like lightning when I heard it. He said that philosophy is irrelevant if it is only about philosophers talking to other philosophers. He said then it is only playing games that will have no effect on the world."

I pressed him about the other major influence on him.

"It was my uncle," he said. "Hasso von Boehmer."

This seemed a surprising choice at first. Von Boehmer was a Nazi officer, a Lieutenant Colonel, in the German army in World War II. But he was one of the July 20, 1944, plotters who tried to assassinate Hitler in the Wolf's Lair in East Prussia. Although he had been immersed in the heady excitement and nationalism of Hitler's rule, he came to realize that it had all gone very wrong and the only right thing to do was to try to stop what was happening. The assassination attempt was the right thing to do, even though it was immensely risky. The plot of course failed and von Boehmer was executed by Hitler loyalists.

"My uncle," Eike-Henner said, "acted on the basis of principle. Hitler had to be stopped. If it cost my uncle his life then that was the price he had to pay. If you have principles then you have to act on them. Otherwise," he repeated, "you are just playing games."

"Is that why you have become involved in the debate on end-of-life issues?" I asked.

"Yes, of course," he answered. "There is a profound ethical issue at the heart of the debate. Are we going to allow people to escape from debilitating illness, when all hope for improvement is gone? Or are we going to make them suffer to the bitter end? And beyond that, are we going to acknowledge that people have autonomy over their own bodies and should be free, with appropriate safeguards, to end their lives when they wish to do so? Able-bodied people can of course do this now (although sometimes they do not know how to do it) but others, some disabled people, cannot. And they are often those who want it most."

"So," I said, "it is an ethical issue for you; you did not want to just write academic papers and give talks at philosophy conferences. You wanted to do something concrete, as you did in the Rodriguez case and in all the various presentations you have made to public bodies. When did you become so interested in these issues?"

"As a young man I was very much on the pro-life side. I opposed abortion, euthanasia and assisted suicide. Even suicide. As a child I had been kept in a postwar Russian labour camp in Eastern Germany. I learned to value life at all costs. But as I began to think about these issues in more depth I began to question them; simply put, these pro-life positions seemed unsupportable by logic. I was torn between the disrespect for life I had seen in the labour camp and what made sense to me. It was a very difficult transition for me, so I can understand why others do not change their views in the way that I did."

"How were you able to change?"

"Probably for lots of reasons. But Schweitzer and von

Boehmer were certainly part of it. If my uncle could give his life to do what was right, I could, and should, drop my beliefs if I thought it was right to do so."

I wanted to find out more about the experiences Eike-Henner had as a youth and how they had affected him. I asked him if he would tell me more about that. He went silent.

"Don't bother with this," I said, "if you do not want to talk about it."

"It is hard to put such an experience into words," he said quietly. "What people see in the news, in areas of conflict are just pictures. They are not reality. It is different when you are imbedded in reality — when you see people being tortured to death, when people are seen as bodies, not persons, when people are used for target practice — my aunt was shot for fun by soldiers while she was swimming in a lake — when people are killed by being tied to tank tracks, when women are raped to death, when a minister is crucified in the doorway of his own church, when people are starving and freezing to death, when you are as vulnerable to being expunged as a worm that might be carelessly trod upon. When you see such things there are two ways you can go: you can decide that life means nothing, or you can decide that life is precious."

"And you?" I asked.

"I came to believe that life is precious. Not that my life is so but that all human life is so. My life was shaped by these experiences, not in a conscious way but initially in an inchoate way, based upon what I had seen. It permeated my world view, and because of that I had strong feelings against abortion and assisted death.

"But then as a young man writing a pro-life book about

abortion I was forced to think about what constitutes being human, and I realized that it is the capacity for sentient cognitive awareness. Can a fetus have that? No it cannot, not until it has developed a brain. Similarly there is no human present after a human's brain dies. There is no awareness then, just a biological organism."

"This was difficult for you to accept?" I asked.

"Very difficult," he answered. "Archimedes said, 'Give me a place to stand and I will move the world.' Well, I had lost my place to stand — a place I had been very sure of. But I was wrong. My views were inconsistent with principles I had. I made a rational decision to restructure my pro-life views. It came at a price, though. An emotional price. But if I did not live according to my views then it is all just games."

* * *

None of the stories told in this book are about people playing games. Each person was driven by compassion and by conscience; each was standing up for what he or she believed to be right. In different ways, each challenged existing law. And if I were a religious person I would say, "God bless them, one and all."

CHAPTER NOTES

INTRODUCTION

For more on the distinctions between various forms of assisted suicide and euthanasia see Eike-Henner Kluge, *Ethics in Health Care: A Canadian Focus* (Toronto: Pearson, 2013).

For commentary on false moral distinctions (and many other things) see Lynn Smith: www.canlii.org/en/bc/bcsc/doc/2012/2012bcsc886/2012bcsc886.html. For example, from article 335:

> *The preponderance of the evidence from ethicists is that there is no ethical distinction between physician-assisted death and other end-of-life practices whose outcome is highly likely to be death. I find the arguments put forward by those ethicists, such as Professor Battin, Dr. Angell and Professor Sumner, to be persuasive.*

On Norman Hope

John Dixon's story about the death of his friend Norman Hope was told in an affidavit he had prepared for the B.C. Supreme Court in the 2011–2012 *Carter et al.* case (see Chapter 6). Dixon was making the point that the BCCLA was a legitimate plaintiff in the case, in addition to the other plaintiffs with direct personal stakes in the matter. Dixon, concerning his friend, wrote:

> *My personal experiences have informed my understanding of why it is often difficult or impossible for dying patients to challenge the*

laws that criminalize physician-assisted dying. In particular, my experience witnessing the death of Norman Hope, a close friend, convinced me that institutional anchors such as the BCCLA are critically important in ensuring that fundamental rights and freedoms are protected . . .

As a practical fact of legal life, if Norman Hope had initiated a challenge to the laws that criminalize physician-assisted dying at the point at which he was diagnosed, there could have been no realistic prospect of his suit being adjudicated before his death. This is the ordinary state of affairs for dying patients who desire medical assistance in easing their passing.

See full affidavit at bccla.org/wp-content/uploads/2012/06/20110830-Affidavit-Carter-BCCLA-Affidavit.pdf.

CHAPTER 1

Note: Some other references given in Appendix 1.

On the Rambergs

I am indebted to John Hofsess, former editor of *Last Rights* magazine, for providing me with a copy of Issue 17 (1998), which contains extensive information on the Ramberg case, including several newspaper reports from the *Calgary Herald* (October 6, 9 and 10 and December 1, 2, 8, 10, 11 and 12, 1941) as well as a transcript of the Coroner's Report, October 10, 1941, and of their preliminary hearing on October 16, 1941.

At the trial, the Rambergs' jury consisted of just six

people (all men): J. DeLisle May, Herbert J. Akitt and Kenneth Denoon, all of Calgary; Graeme Broatch of Cochrane; Kenneth Carlyle of Hubalta; and Leroy Koefoed of Gleichen. The judge was Justice S. J. Sheperd.

At that time juries in Alberta consisted of only six people, the only jurisdiction in Canada with any number of jurors other than twelve. In 1969 Alberta switched to twelve as well.

A. L. (Art) Smith, counsel for Dorothy Ramberg, went on to a distinguished career in politics. He was elected as a Conservative to Parliament in 1945 where he served until 1951, when he resigned due to ill health. He died later that year. While Commons rules allowed that tributes be paid only to members who die while being members of Parliament, by unanimous consent an exception was made in Smith's case and Speaker Ross Macdonald was asked to send a message to Mrs. Smith and the family expressing the "deep sympathy of his fellow Parliamentarians." Liberal Prime Minister Louis St. Laurent spoke of Parliament's "lasting admiration for a dear friend, a great lawyer and a great Parliamentarian." The *Calgary Herald*, in an editorial on December 19, 1951, stated:

> *It seemed there wasn't anybody in Calgary who Art Smith didn't know and who didn't like Art Smith . . . It was what made him the great man he was, an almost incredibly wide and intimate contact with people plus the brilliant and penetrating mind which enabled him to bring humanity . . . into the House of Commons.*

In the same way, some years before, he brought humanity to the trial of the Rambergs.

The Ramberg case was an example of justice being achieved through jury nullification of the law. For more on this little-known and suppressed right of juries, see Gary Bauslaugh, *The Secret Power of Juries* (Toronto: Lorimer, 2013).

Like some parents who lose a child, Dorothy Ramberg never fully recovered from her ordeal with Victor Christopher. She not only had the terrible trauma of dealing with the sick child, she felt responsible for his illness. Someone, probably a well-meaning doctor, told her that the boy's cancer was probably due to a genetic defect carried by his mother. This remark, probably as casual as it was dubious, drastically affected Dorothy's life. She was determined not to get pregnant again, likely affecting her relationship with her husband. She became depressed and alcoholic and took her own life in February of 1961 at the age of forty-seven. She used the same method she and her husband had used to end the life of their son (carbon monoxide), and was taken to the same hospital in Calgary, where she was pronounced dead.

Victor was not so drastically affected and tried to put the tragedy behind him. He married again, but did keep, for a while, a collection of framed photographs of the boy. Each had a letter sealed behind the photos that contained a message from Dorothy to her son. One called him her "dear little lamb" and said she "was sorry she had not died with him." Eventually Victor threw all these reminders away.

On George and Elsie Davis

See *Last Rights*, Issue 17 (1998), which includes 1942 newspaper reports from the *Winnipeg Free Press* on July 17, 22, 23 and 28; and October 5, 7, and 8.

On Eerkiyoot
See *Pittsburg Press*, September 10, 1949, p. 11.

For an excellent commentary on the Inuit prosecutions see Russel Ogden, "Death Hastening and Canada's Inuit," *Last Rights*, Issue 15 (undated but probably 1996).

On Ron Brown and Ronald Lambert
See www.ccdonline.ca/en/humanrights/endoflife/latimer/1997/01.

On Lois Wilson and Victor Hayes
See five newspaper articles located, using ProQuest, on the Canadian Newsstand database: The *Ottawa Citizen*, April 10, 1986, p. A15; The *Montreal Gazette*, April 10, 1986, p. A2; The *Globe and Mail*, April 10, 1986, p. A20; The *Toronto Star*, April 10, 1986, p. A2; The *Toronto Star*, January 8, 1986, p. F14.

On Nancy B
See lawjournal.mcgill.ca/userfiles/other/4827919-Dickens.pdf.

On Jean and Cecil Brush
See www.parl.gc.ca/content/sen/committee/351/euth/rep/lad-a2-e.htm.

CHAPTER 2

For detailed references for the Latimer story, see Gary Bauslaugh, *Robert Latimer: A Story of Justice and Mercy* (Toronto: Lorimer, 2010).

On Latimer's character

Latimer was described by Chief Justice Bayda of Saskatchewan, who had known Latimer for over twenty years, as "a nurturing, caring, giving, respectful, law-abiding responsible parent." See 1995 CanLII 3993 (SKC.A.), or Gary Bauslaugh, *Robert Latimer* (above), for Bayda's whole, much longer quote.

Recent news about Robert Latimer

My book about Latimer (noted above) was the end of our friendship. After working with me on earlier drafts he suddenly withdrew his support after I told him that the book, which was previously planned to include Evelyn Martens's story as well, was going to be just about him. I talked to him a couple of times after that but it was strained and uncomfortable. He stopped answering my emails.

I was gratified by a generally favourable reaction to the book. Kim Campbell, a former federal Justice Minister and Prime Minister, wrote:

> *Robert Latimer's story is the ultimate antidote to the tendency to see the law in abstract terms. The supposed virtue of our legal system is its ability to temper law with justice. This book sets out clearly the many barriers to that goal — naiveté of accused, pop-psychology misconceptions, prosecutorial zeal, professional incompetence, uninformed and biased political and media pressure — among many others. Gary Bauslaugh has written a book that should be on every law school curriculum and on every politician's and justice professional's reading list. The questions he raises about end-of-life issues deserve wide debate, but at the end of the day, as*

the Latimer case illustrates, even if we do change our laws, we will always need to find justice for those good people who are on the wrong side of the law for the right reasons . . . this is an important book. Your own personality comes through in just the right way. You have done a great service in writing the book but I understand Latimer's reticence. Still, with your book, he and his family don't have to ever say anything more.

I was particularly pleased with this because Campbell recognized that at its core the book is deeply sympathetic to and supportive of Latimer and his family.

As one would expect, however, there was also a very hostile reaction to my book from opponents to euthanasia. Seeking ways to put down the book, a number of them seized on the fact that Latimer did not want the book and called it an "unauthorized biography." I was amused by this, wondering if they would have been more favourably disposed to a book authorized by the man they so despised!

A couple of documentary filmmakers talked to me about a Latimer documentary. I did phone him about that, but he absolutely refused to cooperate on such a project. I thought it would bring attention to the legal issues in his case, such as the blocking of giving important information to the jury and the atrocious behavior of the Parole Board, but Latimer was just not interested. It was very difficult to get funding for the film without his participation, so it never happened.

In my book on Latimer I wrote about how the Parole Board of Canada treated him disrespectfully and unfairly from the first time he appeared before them to apply for day parole, and how this continued after he got full parole. It continues today.

Latimer was given a life sentence, which means he is on parole for life, something that entails certain restrictions. For one thing, he is not allowed to travel out of the country without permission.

On June 13, 2013, the Parole Board denied Latimer's request to travel to South America to do some volunteer work. The grounds given were that he posed a risk to the safety of other people. Latimer's lawyer Jason Gratl launched an appeal, but it was denied by the Appeal Division of the Parole Board. But Gratl was not finished. He took the case to the Federal Court, which, on September 16, 2014, found the appeal decision to be unreasonable, and ordered a new review. This time the Appeal Division decided, on February 26, 2015, to approve Latimer's request. The process took almost two years, and was only successful because of the excellent and determined work of Gratl.

CHAPTER 3

The quote from Svend Robinson was reported in The *Windsor Star*, December 8, 2014.

For details on life of Sue Rodriguez: see Helma Libick, "Remembering Sue," in *Last Rights*, Issue 13 (Fall 1994).

For details of Sue Rodriguez's early illness, seeking help, and pledge: see John Hofsess, "Who Cares?" in *Last Rights*, Issue 6 (Oct.–Nov. 1992).

The book read by Rodriguez: Derek Humphry, *Final Exit* (New York: Dell,1992; 3rd. ed., 2002).

For the Rodriguez ruling, see *Rodriguez v. British Columbia* (1993) 3 SCR 519; and Margaret Smith, "The Rodriguez Case," Law and Government Division (October 1993)   publications.gc.ca/Collection-R/LoPBdP/BP/bp349-e.htm

For comments in 2004 by Frank Iacobucci: www.ottawa-menscentre.com/news/20040622Iacobucci.htm.

Commentary from the Special Senate Committee on Euthanasia and Assisted Suicide: www.parl.gc.ca/content/sen/committee/351/euth/rep/lad-a2-e.htm#l

For a challenge to Justice Sopinka's interpretation of Section 7, see Jocelyn Downie, *Dying Justice* (Toronto: University of Toronto Press, 2004).

A commentary on SCC Hearing on *Rodriguez* based on a transcript of the hearing is available at SCC-CSC.gc.ca

For more on Section 1 of the *Charter* and how its applicability is determined (the Oakes test) see The Ontario Justice Education Network: ojen.ca/resource/980.

For the Catholic position on ending life, see *The Catholic Encyclopedia* website at www.newadvent.org/cathen/07441 a.htm

On the split between Hofsess and Rodriguez: www.theinterim.com/issues/euthanasia-suicide/sue-rodriguez-fires-hofsess/

The Special prosecutor's report is attached to a news release by the B.C. Ministry of the Attorney General, June 28, 1995.

Wayne Sumner's article, "The Morgentaler Effect," is in *The Walrus* (January/February 2011).

On jury nullification, see Gary Bauslaugh, *The Secret Power of Juries* (Toronto: Lorimer, 2013).

CHAPTER 4

Much of the information recorded here is from personal conversations between the author, John Hofsess, Russel Ogden and Eike-Henner Kluge.

For information on the history of the Right to Die

Society: www.righttodie.ca/aboutus.html, and John Hofsess, "Educating the world about choice-in-dying," *Last Rights*, Issue 14 (1995).

About John Hofsess and his interest in the right to die: John Hofsess, "Candle in the Wind," in *Homemaker's Magazine* (Nov./Dec. 1991).

Regarding aiding and abetting, the Supreme Court of Canada made the following ruling in *R. v Briscoe*, 2010 SCC 13, [2010] 1 S.C.R. 411:

> *While it is common to speak of aiding and abetting together, the two concepts are distinct, and liability can flow from either one. Broadly speaking . . . aid means to assist or help the actor . . . To abet includes encouraging, instigating, promoting or procuring the crime to be committed.*

For *Of Life and Death*, the report of the Special Senate Committee on Euthanasia and Assisted Suicide: www.parl.gc.ca/content/sen/committee/351/euth/rep/lad-e.htm.

Also see Eike-Henner Kluge, *Ethics in Health Care: A Canadian Focus* (Toronto: Pearson, 2013).

Some recent news about John Hofsess
I did not meet John Hofsess until January of 2015, long after his activities described in Chapter 4. He was reclusive, in his later life at least. A number of people who had known him did not seem to like him or trust him very much, but I could never find out exactly why this was so. I believe there was some feeling that he should have stood by Evelyn Martens when she was arrested, instead of disappearing, but what could he have done for her? If he were to testify on

her behalf what could he say that might help? Her lawyers
called no witnesses anyway and would not have called him.
But the prosecution might well have called him, if he had
been around. This would have put him in an impossible
situation. He alluded to this once, wondering what he would
have done if asked to testify under oath. John was a man
willing to break the law when innocent people are made to
suffer because of a bad law. But he was not a man inclined to
dishonesty. He would have found it difficult or even impossible to tell anything but the truth if called as a witness, and
the truth could well have led to Martens's conviction. So it
may not have been just for his own safety that he went out
of sight during the trial of Evelyn Martens. It was the best
thing he could have done for her.

At the same time, John had his supporters. They include
Margaret Atwood, Canada's leading literary figure, and
Eike-Henner Kluge, Canada's leading bioethicist. John,
in his day, was certainly a courageous figure, genuinely
disturbed by the unpleasant way some people had to die,
devoted to the cause of helping them, willing to risk his own
freedom to do so.

CHAPTER 5

Information about Evelyn Martens's life comes from discussions between her and the author, and information regarding
her trial comes from my attendance at that trial. Also see
Gary Bauslaugh, "The Trial of Evelyn Martens," in *Humanist
Perspectives* no. 152 (Spring 2005).

For the Leenen case: www.canlii.org/en/on/onsc/doc/2
000/2000canlii22380/2000canlii22380.html. Also see Gary
Bauslaugh, "When Trusted Information Sources go Wrong,"
Humanist Perspectives no. 161 (Summer 2007).

On Evelyn Marten's death: A few years after her 2004 trial Evelyn Martens suffered a heart attack, and she passed away on January 2, 2011, a week before her eightieth birthday.

CHAPTER 6

For information about Craig Jones and the B.C. Attorney General's threats, see *Farewell Foundation Newsletters*, October 4 and 7, 2011.

For biographical information on Justice Lynn Smith, see www.cba.org/cba/cle/PDF/Constit09_Smith_bio.pdf

Complete details and documentation of the B.C. Supreme Court case are at the web site for the B.C. Civil Liberties Association: bccla.org/our-work/blog/death-with-dignity-case.

The ruling by Justice Smith, including the proposed safeguards by plaintiff lawyers Arvay and Tucker, in articles 874 to 880, is at bccla.org/wp-content/uploads/2012/06/Carter-v-Canada-AG-2012-BCSC-886.pdf.

CHAPTER 7

For the timeline for the SARS epidemic, see en.wikipedia.org/wiki/Timeline_of_the_SARS_outbreak.

Low's posthumous video is at www.cbc.ca/news/canada/toronto/sars-doctor-donald-low-s-posthumous-plea-for-assisted-suicide-1.1866332.

For the CBC quote about the government's "no intention" see the Low video: www.cbc.ca/news/canada/toronto/sars-doctor-donald-low-s-posthumous-plea-for-assisted-suicide-1.1866332.

Maureen Taylor comments a year later: www.ctvnews.ca/health/i-m-still-grieving-widow-of-assisted-suicide-advocate-dr-donald-low-says-1.1975135.

For Sopinka's quote from the *Rodriguez* decision, see *Rodriguez v. British Columbia* (1993) 3 SCR 519.

For Smith's quotes for the old policy at [274]: bccla.org/wp-content/uploads/2012/06/Carter-v-Canada-AG-2012-BCSC-886.pdf.

For the new policy as of December 2014, see policybase. cma.ca/dbtw-wpd/CMAPolicy/PublicB.htm and search for "assisted death."

For a report on Ottawa CMA meeting, August 2014, see o.canada.com/news/national/canadian-doctors-want-freedom-to-choose-whether-to-help-terminal-patients-die.

CHAPTER 8

For more details on federal/provincial responsibilities in health and health care, see www.parl.gc.ca/content/lop/researchpublications/prb0858-e.htm.

For a review of the timeline for Bill 52, see www.montreal-gazette.com/health/Bill+timeline/9510618/story.html.

CHAPTER 9

For information on the number of suicides in Canada: www.med.uottawa.ca/sim/data/Suicide_e.htm.

For Gillian's letter and some personal information: www.deadatnoon.com.

Other details in this chapter taken from interviews the author had with Jonathan Bennett.

A note on the costs of care for the elderly

One of Gillian's main points should get special attention here, because it concerns a matter that is often avoided by advocates for dying with dignity. It is the matter of the costs of keeping the elderly alive. While this, in a rational world, ought to be of major concern in the debates about end-of-life matters, it is avoided essentially for political reasons. If one tries to point out the high costs of, as Gillian puts it, keeping carcasses alive, one is branded as a supporter of "death panels" and enforced euthanasia — ridding the world of those who are no longer productive, even threatening the imperfect and the disabled.

But it is important to separate the hysterical responses to this matter from the rational. It is vitally important that we as a society most strongly resist any suggestion that euthanasia be forced on anyone who wishes to continue to live. Virtually all parties in this debate agree with this. In fact those who support the right-to-die movement are often more rigorous in their thinking about this than are many of the most vocal opponents of any progressive change in assisted suicide and euthanasia laws: they oppose capital punishment — a kind of enforced involuntary euthanasia.

It remains the case, however, that there are many people who, toward the end of their lives, no longer want to be a burden to family, friends and society in general. This is not a matter of being pressured to end their lives (which can happen and must be carefully guarded against) but legitimately not wanting to go on with the indignities of helplessness and uselessness. Others may want life to continue for as long as possible, in whatever condition they may be, and that must be their unquestioned right. But many people do not want a degraded life, and that too must be their absolute right, which in fact it is according to Canadian law. Suicide is legal, but has not been available to those who need assistance in ending life in a dignified way. Gillian knew what to do and how to do it, but even she was leery about having her children present, lest they be somehow implicated.

The cost of keeping themselves alive is a perfectly proper and reasonable concern for those suffering with terminal illness. Recognizing that the money involved could be used to help others is an honourable reason to opt for dying, so long as that is the unforced, genuine view of the dying person himself or herself. Like Gillian, we should not shun this one legitimate reason for choosing to die, and indeed for allowing assistance in dying.

Public health care spending per person in 2008 was under $3,000 up to the age of about sixty, and then rose steeply to over $20,000 for those over eighty-five. See the Library of Parliament research publication at www.parl.gc.ca/Content/LOP/ResearchPublications/2011-122-e.htm.

A note of explanation about Gillian's reference to a "Ponzi" scheme:
The term is usually used to refer to investment practices that, often starting as legitimate plans, cannot deliver on promises made by investors and begin to inflate returns by using the contributions of new investors. Eventually, when insufficient new investors can be found to cover the mounting deficits, the scheme collapses, often with investors losing much or all of their investments. In regard to the costs of caring for the aged and infirm, to which Gillian was referring, this could be covered through tax revenue when sufficient numbers of young people were coming into the system to pay taxes to cover medical costs for everyone. But, as with a Ponzi scheme, the balance is lost when there are too many old people and too few new contributors to cover the increasing costs. The parallel is not exact, however, because a Ponzi scheme involves misappropriation of funds: new investors' money being used to pay old ones. In

health care, tax revenue is intended to pay for health costs but those costs, when the proportion of the infirm elderly becomes too high, threaten to overwhelm the capacity of the system.

CHAPTER 10

See transcript of the hearing, available at: www.scc-csc. gc.ca/case-dossier/info/search-recherche-eng.aspx

Supreme Court Justices at October 15, 2014, hearing on assisted suicide, with sample references
Beverly McLachlin (Chief Justice): www. thecanadianencyclopedia.ca/en/article/beverley-mclachlin.

Rosalie Abella: www.theglobeandmail.com/news/ national/justice-tempered-with-a-soft-heart/article1198847.

Thomas Cromwell: www.cbc.ca/news/canada/thomas-cromwell-sworn-in-as-new-supreme-court-judge-1.828507.

Clément Gascon: www.ctvnews.ca/politics/meet-clement-gascon-the-unvetted-quebec-judge-joining-the-scc-1.2041096.

Andromache Karakatsanis: news.nationalpost.com/full-comment/christie-blatchford-some-star-power-for-our-top-court.

Louis Lebel: www.thestar.com/news/canada/2014/11/29/ supreme_court_justice_louis_lebel_retires_sunday.html.

Michael Moldaver: news.nationalpost.com/full-comment/national-post-editorial-board-a-land-without-Borking and news.nationalpost.com/full-comment/ christie-blatchford-some-star-power-for-our-top-court.

Marshall Rothstein: metronews.ca/news/canada/1369654/ supreme-court-justice-marshall-rothstein-bids-an-impromptu-public-farewell.

Richard   Wagner: www.ctvnews.ca/canada/
new-supreme-court-justice-pays-tribute-to-hero-father-at-
swearing-in-1.1063769.

CHAPTER 11

The   ruling: scc-csc.lexum.com/scc-csc/scc-csc/en/item/
14637/index.do.

BCCLA press release (the quoted material was taken from
an earlier, similar press release): bccla.org/news/2015/02/
release-bccla-wins-historic-death-with-dignity-case-at-
supreme-court-of-canada.

Euthanasia Prevention Coalition's statement: www.epcc.
ca/press-releases.

CHAPTER 12

Information about Willowbrook: willowbrookstateschool.
blogspot.ca/p/history.html.

Information about the Allan Memorial Institute and
Dr. Cameron: coat.ncf.ca/our_magazine/links/issue43/
articles/1957_1961_canada.htm.

APPENDIX 1
CATALOGUE OF CANADIAN LEGAL CASES INVOLVING ASSISTED SUICIDE AND EUTHANASIA

In preparing a catalogue of cases of assisted death in Canada one runs into all sorts of questionable cases. I have left out dubious cases where depressed parents thought their children would be better off dead; these are pathological events and have no moral justification whatsoever. But a parent ending the life of a child in hopeless physical misery, as in the cases of the Rambergs and Robert Latimer, is an act of love and compassion. I do include such genuine cases of mercy killing.

I do not include cases that are better judged to be murder, although the distinction is not always clear. I have also left out cases where death is brought on by refusal for religious reasons to get treatment, or by people deluded by medical frauds.

Note: acronyms at the end of each example (RTD, LR etc.) relate to sources at end of this appendix.

1941 — In Alberta, Victor and Dorothy Ramberg used carbon monoxide to end the life of their two-year-old son dying of cancer. They were charged with murder but found not guilty (see Chapter 1, also RTD, LR).

1942 — In Manitoba, George Davis ended the life of his suffering wife and was acquitted of a murder charge (see Chapter 1, also RTD).

1949 — In the Northwest Territories, Inuit men Eerkiyoot and Ishakak were prosecuted and found guilty of aiding the suicide of Eerkiyoot's mother. Eerkiyoot was given one year and released after six months, and Ishakak was given a suspended sentence (see Chapter 1, also RTD, LR).

1955 — In the Northwest Territories, Inuit man Kaotok was charged with murder in the death of his father, Kitigi-tok. The father, an old man, was shot to death on a hunting trip with his son. Kaotok claimed that he assisted in his father's suicide, although authorities suspected murder. The jury declared Kaotok not guilty, based on lack of evidence (LR).

1963 — In the Northwest Territories, Inuit men Amah, Avinga and Nangmalik were found guilty of assisting the suicide of their fatally ill chief, who shot himself. Sentence was suspended (RTD, LR).

1977 — In Manitoba, Ron Brown smothered an eleven-year-old boy who appeared to be terminally ill. Shortly afterwards Brown confessed to his superior but the incident was not reported for nineteen years when, in 1997,

Brown was convicted of manslaughter and given a two-year sentence (see Chapter 1, also RTD, CHN).

1982 — In Alberta, Dr. Nachum Gal, a pediatric resident, was charged with first-degree murder of a severely brain-damaged baby. Gal fled to Israel and attempts to extradite him failed. Two nurses who were involved were suspended for a year (Downie, RTD, CHN).

1985 — In Quebec, Bruno Bergeron killed his ninety-four-year-old wife with an axe. She was suffering from Alzheimer's, congestive heart failure, anemia and diabetes. He pleaded guilty to murder and was given a suspended sentence (RTD, CHN).

1986 — In Ontario, Lois Wilson pleaded guilty to "aiding and abetting suicide" of her boyfriend Victor Hayes, who thought he had stomach cancer. Sentenced to six months (see Chapter 1, also RTD, LR).

1990 — In British Columbia, David Lewis was initially charged with murder in the deaths of eight people with AIDS, but the charges were withdrawn after the coroner decided there was not enough evidence to justify the charges (RTD).

1991 — In Ontario, the son of a man dying of cancer turned up the infusion rate of morphine, presumably to hasten the man's death. A nurse discovered this and turned it back down, but the son was charged with attempted murder. He pleaded guilty to mischief likely to endanger life and was put on probation (Downie).

1991 — In Ontario, nurse Scott Mataya gave a lethal injection to a seriously ill cancer patient. He was initially charged with first-degree murder but then entered a guilty plea to a lesser charge of administering a noxious substance. Mataya was given a suspended sentence and ordered to give up his nursing license (see Chapter 12, also Downie, DWD, CHN).

1992 — In Quebec, a doctor gave a patient dying of AIDS a lethal injection of potassium chloride, at the patient's request. The provincial professional physician's association disciplined the doctor but successfully recommended against criminal charges on the grounds that he did what was best for the patient and that if charged a jury would not convict him anyway (Downie).

1992 — In Quebec, twenty-five-year-old Nancy B., suffering from a disabling neurological condition known Guillain-Barré syndrome, was granted permission to end treatment, and to have a doctor's help in dying peacefully (see Chapter 1, SSC, MLJ).

1993 — In Ontario, physician Dr. Alberto de la Rocha gave a lethal potassium chloride injection to a seriously ill cancer patient. He was initially charged with second-degree murder, then pleaded guilty to administering a noxious substance and was given a three-year suspended sentence. Again the courts were concerned that a jury would not find the respected de la Rocha guilty (See Chapter 12, also Downie, DWD, RTD, CHN).

1993 — In British Columbia, Sue Rodriguez's petition to have assistance in dying was denied. MP Svend Robinson was investigated for assisted suicide but not charged (see Chapter 3).

1993 — In Saskatchewan Robert Latimer was charged with and convicted of the murder of his twelve-year-old daughter Tracy (see Chapter 2).

1994 — In Nova Scotia, Cheryl Myers and her husband Michael Power were charged with second-degree murder after fulfilling a promise made to her father to kill him when he could no longer care for himself and was in great pain. They smothered him with a pillow. They pleaded guilty to manslaughter, were given suspended sentences and placed on probation for three years, and were directed to do 150 hours of community service (Downie, CHN).

1994 — In Ontario, Jean Brush killed her husband Cecil and was given a suspended sentence (see Chapter 1, Downie, CHN, SSC).

1994 — In Alberta, Robert Cashin was charged with attempted murder in the death of his sixty-nine-year-old terminally ill mother. Allegedly he put a large number of pills in her hand and she swallowed them. She died three days later. Cashin pleaded guilty to administering a noxious substance and was given a suspended sentence and two years of probation (RTD, CHN).

1995 — In Nova Scotia, Mary Fogarty was convicted for assisting the suicide of her friend Brenda Barnes, after allegedly providing her with syringes and insulin and helping her write a suicide note. Fogarty was sentenced to three years probation and three hundred hours of community service. The jury concluded that Fogarty had acted out of self-interest, since she was a beneficiary of Barnes's estate. This was the first conviction for assisted suicide since the Inuit cases of the 1940s, '50s and '60s and Lois Wilson in 1986, and not a usual case of assisted suicide because of the inheritance issue (Downie, CHN).

1996 — In Quebec, Danielle Blais ended the life of her six-year-old autistic son. The initial charge of first-degree murder was reduced to manslaughter. She was found guilty and given a suspended sentence (RTD, CHN).

1996 — In Ontario, Dr. Maurice Généreux was charged with aiding and abetting suicide, counselling to commit suicide, criminal negligence causing death and criminal negligence causing bodily harm. The charges concerned two HIV positive patients, one of whom ultimately did commit suicide, and the other who attempted to do so. Généreux falsified the death certificate of the patient who died. In December of 1997, Généreux pleaded guilty to assisting suicide and became the first doctor on Canada to be so convicted. In May 1998 he was sentenced to two years less a day plus three years probation for providing lethal drugs to two nonterminal patients. The prosecutors may have been particularly aggressive in this case because Généreux was known by prosecutors to have had a previous conviction for a sexual offence (Downie, CHN).

1997 — In Nova Scotia, Dr. Nancy Morrison was charged with first-degree murder for ending the life of a terminally ill patient, Paul Mills, who was dying of cancer of the esophagus. After various attempts to relive his pain, Dr. Morrison injected him with potassium chloride. The judge ruled that a jury was unlikely to convict, and discharged the case (see Chapter 12, also Downie, DWD, CHN).

1997 — In Manitoba, Bert Doerksen was suspected of assisting the suicide of his wife, using carbon monoxide. Charges were dropped as Doerksen himself was near death and would have had to attend court on a stretcher (RTD, CHN).

1999 — In Ontario, Wayne Hussey was found not guilty of assisted suicide after he had test-fired a gun that his father later used to kill himself (RTD).

2000 — In Quebec, Herbert Lerner suffocated his wife with a plastic bag. She was in the early stages of Alzheimer's. He pleaded guilty to manslaughter and was given a five-year sentence. Lerner committed suicide a year later (RTD, CHN).

2002 — In Quebec, Alain Quimper pleaded guilty to second-degree murder after strangling his mother, who was terminally ill with Alzheimer's. Quimper then beat some of the attendants at the mother's home with a metal bar. He was given life imprisonment without eligibility for parole for fourteen years (RTD, CHN).

2003 — In British Columbia, Julianna Zsiros was found guilty in the death of her housemate, after showing her how to start her car and ensuring the garage where the car was located was airtight. The housemate died of carbon monoxide poisoning. Zsiros was given a suspended sentence (RTD).

2004 — In Quebec, Marielle Houle was charged with aiding and abetting the suicide of her thirty-six-year-old son, Charles Fariala, who was in the early stages of multiple sclerosis. She pleaded guilty and was given a suspended sentence with three years probation (see Chapter 12, also DWD, RTD, CHN).

2004 — In British Columbia, Evelyn Martens of the Right to Die Society of Canada was charged with and acquitted on two charges of assisting suicide. This was the first prosecution in Canada based on an organizational assistance of suicide (see Chapter 5).

2004 — In Manitoba, eighty-six-year-old Tony Jaworski ended the life of his wife, who was suffering from colon cancer and advanced Alzheimer's. He pleaded guilty to manslaughter and was given three years probation (RTD).

2005 — In Quebec, André Bergeron was charged with the attempted murder of his wife, Marielle Gagnon, who was suffering from Friedreich's ataxia. Two attempts to end her life failed. Bergeron was given a suspended sentence, with three years' probation, for aggravated assault (DWD, RTD, CHN).

2006 — In Ontario, Raymond Kirk was given a suspended sentence and three years' probation for aiding the suicide of his wife, who was suffering from great back pain that doctors could not relieve (DWD).

2007 — In British Columbia, Dr. Ramesh Kumar Sharma was sentenced to two years less a day of community service for assisting the suicide of ailing ninety-three-year-old Roth Wolfe (DWD, RTD, CHN).

2007 — In Nova Scotia, the RCMP decided not to lay charges against those involved in suicide of Elizabeth MacDonald, a Canadian with multiple sclerosis who travelled to Switzerland to die with the organization Dignitas (DWD, TS).

2008 — In Quebec, Stéphan Dufour assisted his uncle, Chantal Maltais, to commit suicide by hanging. Maltais was suffering from the effects of polio and had serious coordination problems. He had asked repeatedly for help in dying. In an apparent case of jury nullification, Dufour was acquitted (DWD, CBC, CHN).

2010 — In Ontario, Peter Fonteece pleaded guilty to criminal negligence in the death of his wife, who died from an overdose of sleeping pills, but was found not guilty of assisting her suicide. Eike-Henner Kluge, in commenting on the death, said that Fonteece should never have been prosecuted because he had no obligation to intervene since her actions in committing suicide were not illegal (DWD, G&M).

June 2012 — The B.C. Civil Liberties Association and three other plaintiffs filed a lawsuit to challenge the laws that criminalize assisted suicide. The B.C. Supreme Court agreed with the plaintiffs, their decision was overturned in the B.C. Court of Appeal, but then affirmed by the Supreme Court of Canada (see Chapters 6, 10 and 11).

SOURCES

CBC: www.cbc.ca/news/canada/montreal/quebec-man-acquitted-on-assisted-suicide-charge-1.737601

Compassionate Health Care Network (CHN) [Note: I do not subscribe to the ideas expressed in this website, but the research is helpful]: www.chninternational.com/history_of_euthanasia_in_canada%20by%20Cheryl%20Eckstein%2007.htm

Globe and Mail: www.theglobeandmail.com/news/national/as-desperation-leads-woman-to-suicide-husbands-fate-hangs-in-balance/article4352522/

Last Rights (LR): Russel Ogden, "Death Hastening and Canada's Inuit," *Last Rights*, Issue 15 (1996).

McGill Law Journal on Nancy B. (MLJ): lawjournal.mcgill.ca/userfiles/other/4827919-Dickens.pdf

Right to Die, Canada (RTD): www.righttodie.ca

The Special Senate Committee on Euthanasia and Assisted Suicide (SSC): www.parl.gc.ca/content/sen/committee/351/euth/rep/lad-a2-e.htm

Toronto Star: www.thestar.com/news/canada/2012/10/20/love_story_ends_with_sick_woman_taking_own_life.html

APPENDIX 2
FAILED ATTEMPTS AT LEGISLATIVE CHANGES

On January 16, 2014, Francine Lalonde, former Bloc Québécois Member of Parliament for La Pointe-de-l'île, Quebec, died after a long struggle with bone cancer. During her seventeen years as an MP Lalonde was best known for her efforts to bring about legislated changes to Canadian laws on assisted suicide.

In 2005 Lalonde introduced private member's Bill C-407, proposing to amend the *Criminal Code of Canada* to allow physician-assisted suicide. The bill failed due to the calling of an election in 2006, and then failed again in 2008 for the same reason.

On May 13, 2009, Lalonde introduced a new version of the bill, Bill C-384, which finally made its way to the floor of the House of Commons for a one-hour debate on October 2, 2009. In that debate Lalonde said:

Mr. Speaker, I first introduced a private member's bill on the right to die with dignity in June 2005, because I felt confident that Quebeckers and Canadians needed Parliament to amend the Criminal Code *to recognize that every person, subject to certain specific conditions, had the right to an end of life that is consistent with the values of dignity and freedom they have always espoused and so that an individual's wish regarding his or her death would be respected. In fact, I introduced this bill so that people would have a choice, the same right to choose that people in other countries have. My conviction has grown stronger, and that is why I am introducing an amended bill on the right to die with dignity, Bill C-384.*

Lalonde's bill proposed that clauses be added to Section 222 of the *Criminal Code*, which defines homicide, the key being that a medical practitioner does not commit homicide "by reason only that he or she aids a person to die with dignity."

In Lalonde's proposal, the person who dies must be at least eighteen years of age and either continue to experience severe physical or mental pain without any prospect of relief, or suffer from a terminal illness.

The person must also appear lucid and have "provided a medical practitioner . . . with two written requests more than ten days apart, expressly stating the person's free and informed consent to die, and have designated in writing, with free and informed consent, before two witnesses with no personal interest in the death of the person, another person to act on his or her behalf with any medical practitioner when the person does not appear to be lucid."

The medical practitioner must also:

- request and receive written confirmation of the diagnosis from another medical practitioner with no personal interest in the death of the person,
- have no reasonable grounds to believe that the written requests were made under duress or while the person was not lucid,
- have informed the person of the consequences of his or her requests and of the alternatives available,
- desist if any time the person changes his or her mind, and
- provide the coroner with a copy of the confirmation of the diagnosis by a second medical practitioner.

Lalonde's bill also proposed that Section 241(b) banning assisted suicide be modified to accommodate the changes to Section 222, decriminalizing physician-assisted suicide.

On March 16, 2010, Lalonde managed to get a second hour of debate on the bill. Sadly, her simple and compassionate proposal received scant support in the House of Commons. After an unpromising debate on the second reading, a vote was taken on April 21, 2010 to send the bill to the Justice and Human Rights committee for further study. It was defeated by a vote of 228 to 59.

* * *

Lalonde's real legacy may be seen in legislative follow-up to the 2015 Supreme Court Ruling overturning the ban on assisted suicide. Perhaps it will come in the form of Bill S-225 "An Act to Amend the Criminal Code (physician-assisted death)," a Senate bill that received second reading in the Senate on December 10, 2014. The provisions of Bill S-225 are similar to but more detailed than Bill C-384.

Yet another private member's bill, Bill C-581, was introduced and given first reading on March 27, 2014, this time sponsored by Steven Fletcher, Conservative from Charleswood—St. James—Assiniboia, Manitoba. Again, C-581 is similar in its thrust to Lalonde's C-384.

Nine earlier attempts to pass assisted death legislation, all private members' bills, all failed:

- Bill C-351: An act to amend the *Criminal Code* (terminally ill persons), introduced in March 1991, passed first reading and then died with prorogation of Parliament.
- Bill C-203: An act to amend the *Criminal Code* (terminally ill persons), introduced in May, 1991, passed first reading and second reading in September 1991, and was passed on to a legislative committee for further consideration, Hearings began on October 29, 1991, and then adjourned indefinitely in February 1992.
- Bill C-261: An act to legalize the administration of euthanasia under certain conditions, introduced in June 1991, passed first reading. In October 1991 it was given second reading and then dropped from the Order Paper.

- Bill C-385: An act to amend the *Criminal Code* (aiding suicide) introduced December 1992, passed first reading and then died on prorogation.
- Bill C-215: An act to amend the *Criminal Code* (aiding suicide), introduced February 1994, passed first reading and then in September 1994 was dropped from the Order Paper.
- Bill S-13: An act to amend the *Criminal Code* (protection of health care workers), introduced by Senator Sharon Carstairs in November 1996, died on prorogation.
- Bill S-29: An act to amend the *Criminal Code* (protection of patients and health care providers), introduced by Senator Thérèse Lavoie-Roux in April 1999, died on prorogation.
- Bill S-2: An act to facilitate the making of legitimate medical decisions regarding life-sustaining treatments and the controlling of pain, introduced by Senator Sharon Carstairs in October 1999, and referred to the Standing Senate Committee on Legal and Constitutional Affairs in February 2000, where it died.
- Bill C-407: An act to amend the *Criminal Code* (right to die with dignity) introduced by Francine Lalonde in June 2005 and given a one-hour reading on October 31, 2005. It died a month later on dissolution of Parliament.

It is often difficult in democratic countries to pass controversial legislation, even when supported by the majority of
people. The ten private members' bills listed above had virtually no chance of success; few private members' bills do. And
no bill proposing the decriminalization of assisted suicide has
ever been sponsored by any Canadian government, except
in Quebec (see Chapter 8), in spite of strong public support.
Our political system, in controversial matters, is often subject
to the tyranny of very vocal and well-organized minorities,
and parties in power feel they will lose more than they gain in
proposing or supporting such legislation.

The same was true in the abortion debate. No party in power
would tackle the law criminalizing abortion, even though that
cruel law was opposed by a majority of Canadians. If it had
not been for the courageous actions of Henry Morgentaler,
we could still have women seeking back-alley abortions.
We could still have doctors being arrested for carrying out
abortions, and women for having them. Henry Morgentaler
defied the law, and his actions ultimately led to a change in
the abortion law. But this was not accomplished by politicians;
the law was changed by the members of the Supreme Court
of Canada who, on looking at the Morgentaler case, declared
the abortion law unconstitutional.

Before our new *Constitution* was passed in Parliament
in 1982, the Supreme Court of Canada was a somewhat
moribund organization without much impact on the lives of
most Canadians. But the *Constitution* and its *Charter of Rights
and Freedoms* changed everything. The laws are still set by
Parliament but the constitutionality of any of those laws can
be challenged, meaning any of them can be struck down by
the Court. So the Court has now become a major player in
application of the law, and it has become a major force for

social change in Canada.

Without the *Constitution* and the authority it gives to the Supreme Court of Canada, we would have a less just and merciful country. Some people object to the power this gives to an unelected body, and critical cries about an "activist" Court exceeding its jurisdiction are heard every time the Court makes a serious decision.

The Court, however, is simply doing what the *Constitution* says it should do, adjudicate the constitutionality of our laws. This duty was not self-assigned by the court; it was specified in the legislation — the *Constitution* — passed by our elected politicians. Wisely, the legislators of the day realized that their job was to set the overall framework for the embodiment of the rights and freedoms we as a country believe in. The principles were established by legislators, but the application of those principles, the legislators realized, should be left in the hands of an impartial legal body.

That is as it should be, in spite of the inevitable shrill complaints from those who disagree with Court decisions. We surely do not want decisions regarding constitutionality of our laws being made by those involved in the political pressures and exigencies of the moment.

SOURCES

Bill C-384: www.parl.gc.ca/HousePublications/Publication.aspx?Docid=3895681

Text of debate on Bill C-384: openparliament.ca/bills/40-3/C-384/

Details on Bill S-225: openparliament.ca/bills/41-2/S-225/

Details on Bill C-581: openparliament.ca/bills/41-2/C-581/

List of other bills: www.parl.gc.ca/Content/LOP/ResearchPublications/2010-68-e.htm

APPENDIX 3
PALLIATIVE SEDATION

The assumption is made in Canada that palliative sedation is neither physician-assisted suicide nor voluntary euthanasia, and it is therefore, apparently, practiced widely in this country. That it is so practiced is a good thing, because the suffering of dying people is thereby relieved.

However, when administered in a manner that hastens death, palliative sedation is a form of voluntary euthanasia. For one thing, an unconscious patient cannot eat or drink, so unless measures are taken to nourish the patient, as well as sedate him or her, then the patient's decline is very likely to be hastened. This is sometimes referred to as "slow euthanasia" — in effect, the intentional ending of a life, though not so quickly as, say, by a lethal injection.

Opponents of assisted death sometimes argue that hydration and nourishment must accompany palliative sedation.

This seems remarkably pointless, simply allowing a patient to survive longer in a stuporous state. It seems unlikely that most doctors would see any point in doing this.

Besides of the effects of lack of food and hydration, it is also the case that death can be hastened by the level of sedative used. Morphine, the most common drug used for palliative sedation (or any other such drug), is fatal if given in a high enough dose. And how is the right dosage to be accurately judged, as enough to cause unconsciousness but not death? It seems very likely that sometimes, at least, death is hastened just by an excess of the sedating drug.

On the other hand many doctors are understandably uncomfortable with the idea that palliative sedation is a form of slow euthanasia. I have heard a doctor flatly deny that it is so. Apparently, it just does not seem to many doctors as the same thing as assisted death, perhaps because the process is more gradual. But surely it is so. One doctor was quoted as saying:

> *I wouldn't feel comfortable giving an injection of potassium [which would be lethal] but I feel okay about increasing the morphine to help the patient die sooner.*

Doctors sometimes cope with this cognitive dissonance about palliative sedation — that the patient may die sooner, but it is not hastening death — by invoking what is called the principle of double effect. In this case the principle states that while there may be two effects of the treatment — relief from pain and hastened death — only the first effect is intended. The morphine is given to reduce pain, but not with the intention of killing. Therefore its administration is not the same as deliberately hastening death. But it is, nonetheless, knowingly hastening death. Is there a significant difference between a deliberate action and a knowing one? I find difficulty seeing a real difference, at least one significant enough to make one form of hastening death (palliative sedation) legal and another — say, lethal injection — murder. However, the difference has been widely accepted by law enforcement authorities, since we do not see prosecutions for palliative sedation.

The principle of double effect is sometimes invoked by the Catholic Church to escape from certain moral conundrums created by some of its absolute doctrines. The absolute prohibition on intentional death, for example, becomes untenable in some circumstances, for example self-defence. The Church does not say that you must just accept, passively, being killed by an attacker; you can defend yourself, even with lethal force if necessary, to save your own life. But if killing is intrinsically morally wrong, as the Church would have it, then killing in self-defence must be intrinsically morally wrong. It is still taking on that which is God's prerogative.

To deal with such logical inconsistency, the Church has often invoked some version of the principle of double effect, that for example in a case of killing in self-defence the primary intention was not to kill the other person but to protect oneself.

But, one might ask, can one be absolved of responsibility for knowingly causing a death simply by stating that the death was not what one was seeking — that it only was a necessary outcome, not the desired one?

The double effect principle has validity only if the second unwanted effect is unknown or uncertain. One for example may take an action that has unknown or unexpected consequences, and in that case responsibility for the outcome might be seen to be lessened. But how can that responsibility be denied if the unwanted result was known and certain?

Unwisely, I think, in writing for the majority decision in the Rodriguez case, Justice Sopinka wrote that giving lethal doses of pain medication is in fact different from assisting suicide:

> *The administration of drugs designed for pain control in dosages which the physician knows will hasten death constitutes active contribution to death by any standard. However, the distinction drawn here is one based on intention — in the case of palliative care the intention is to ease pain, which has the effect of hastening death, while in the case of assisted suicide the intention is undeniably to cause death . . . In my view, distinctions based on intent are important, and in fact form the basis of our criminal law.*

There is an error in thinking here — on the part of Sopinka and on the part of many doctors who feel justified in their actions because of good intentions. Note that I am not arguing that doctors are wrong to do what they do; I am glad that they do administer palliative sedation, shortening the misery of terminal illness, when they do. It is just that their defence for breaking the law, and Sopinka's support for that defence, does not stand up to logical scrutiny. I can appreciate their attempts to justify what is undoubtedly, in virtually all cases, a humane action, but I am uncomfortable with a justification that is logically unsound.

Yes, intentions are important in law. Suppose a doctor gave a patient a pain medication that happened, to no one's knowledge, to conflict with other medications the same patient was taking, and the patient dies. This would not be murder or any sort of offence unless it could shown that the doctor was careless in prescribing this pain-relieving drug. The intention of giving the new medicine was to relieve pain, not to kill the patient. The law would recognize that. But suppose the doctor knew of the conflict of medications and still administered the fatal drug? Could the doctor then argue that his intention was just to relieve pain, even though he knew the patient would die? No sensible system of justice would accept such claims of intention, where a fatal outcome was known and certain.

All of these medical and legal gyrations are necessary only because we have, in the past, chosen to make physician-assisted death illegal. If euthanasia is made legal, as is proposed in Quebec, then palliative sedation becomes a straightforward extension of that idea. Doctors would administer palliative sedation with the intention of both easing pain and, in some cases at least, shortening life. The process of palliative sedation would be brought into the open and countenanced, and suitable controls and oversight could be introduced.

SOURCES

Quote from a doctor regarding increasing morphine to help a patient die, and other similar quotes: J. A. Billings and S. D. Block, *Journal of Palliative Care* 12.4 (Winter 1996). Reprinted in *Last Rights*, Issue 17 (1998).

On Sopinka and the double effect: *Rodriguez v. British Columbia* (1993) 3 SCR 607.

APPENDIX 4
OTHER COUNTRIES

As of spring 2015, some form of assisted death is available in the following jurisdictions (most of this information was compiled by Justice Lynn Smith in *Carter v. Canada*). At the time of this writing, many other states and countries are considering more progressive legislation.

1) Oregon

The Oregon *Death with Dignity Act*, the first of its kind in North America, was passed in a state-wide vote (Measure 16) on November 8, 1994, with a 51% majority. The legislation allows for a very limited form of physician-assisted dying: the provision of a prescription for a lethal dosage of drugs that can then be self-administered by the patient.

The following criteria must be applied; the patient must be:

- over the age of eighteen,
- a resident of Oregon,
- be capable (as confirmed by two witnesses),
- be diagnosed by both the attending and a consulting physician to be suffering from a terminal disease (likely to die within six months), and
- have voluntarily expressed in writing his or her wish to die.

There are various other safeguards built into the procedure, such as the requirement for two oral requests for the medication and one written one over a period of fifteen days. There are several other requirements of the attending physician, such as fully informing the patient about his or her condition and advising the patient about other alternatives. If the patient appears to be depressed, or otherwise mentally unstable, the physician must refer the patient for counselling.

The Oregon Health Division is charged with complying with the *Act* and compiling documentation in that regard. In 2010 there were ninety-six lethal prescriptions given out and there were sixty-five suicides carried out using the prescribed drugs (some of these were issued in earlier years). Of ten thousand deaths in Oregon in 2010, about twenty-one were from the prescribed drugs.

2) Washington State
Washington State voters passed Initiative 1000, the *Death With Dignity Act* on November 4, 2008, with a 58% vote. It is very similar to the Oregon act, and has similar numbers of participants.

3) Montana

Montana has no legislation legalizing assisted suicide, but in 2009 the state Supreme Court ruled that if a mentally competent, terminally ill patient requests and is granted a physician's assistance in dying, that physician will not be held criminally liable.

4) Vermont

In May of 2013 Vermont passed legislation similar to that in Oregon.

5) New Mexico

In January 2014 a judge in New Mexico ruled that terminally ill patients who are mentally competent have the right to have physician-assisted dying.

6) The Netherlands

The Termination of Life on Request and Assisted Suicide Act (the Dutch act) was passed and came into force in the Netherlands in 2002. The act did not in general decriminalize these actions, but made exceptions for physicians under certain circumstances. It really just codified practices and judicial decisions that had emerged over the previous thirty years.

There is no distinction made between assisted suicide and euthanasia, and euthanasia is used as a general term to cover both practices.

Under the Dutch act, a physician who carries out euthanasia is exempt from prosecution, but the physician must:

- be satisfied that the patient's request is voluntary and carefully considered,
- be satisfied that the patient's suffering is unbearable with no hope of improvement,

- have fully informed the patient,
- have come to the conclusion, with the patient, that there is no other reasonable alternative,
- have consulted at least one other independent physician who can confirm in writing the above conditions are in place, and
- end the life with due medical care and attention.

There are five Regional Review Committees (RRCs) that review all cases of euthanasia, and over the years have added some more procedural requirements, such as staying with the patient until death occurs. The RRCs must have an uneven number of participants and include a physician, a legal expert and an ethicist. Each case of euthanasia must be reported to a RRC, which must then decide if there are grounds for criminal prosecution — that is, if the conditions set out in the Dutch act have not been met. The RRCs issue annual reports of their deliberations.

All cases of euthanasia must originate in a request from a patient, and no doctor is required to comply.

In 2005, when detailed studies were carried out, there were 136,402 deaths in the Netherlands, and 8,400 requests for assisted death of which 2,425 were granted — 2,325 for euthanasia and 100 for assisted suicide.

7) Belgium

On May 28, 2002, the Belgian act on euthanasia was passed, coming into effect in September of that year. It was based on and is very similar to the Dutch act, with some provisions spelled out in more detail. The Belgian act specifies only euthanasia, but it is understood that this includes physician-assisted suicide.

The Belgian oversight board is the sixteen-member Federal Control and Evaluation Commission (FCEC), which reviews in detail all cases of euthanasia. If two-thirds of the Commission believe that the required conditions have not been fulfilled the matter is turned over to a public prosecutor. The FCEC also prepares biannual reports with detailed statistics and recommendations, if any.

In 2007 there were 100,658 deaths in Belgium, of which 495 were euthanasia.

8) Switzerland

There is no specific statute on assisted suicide or euthanasia in Switzerland, but these are covered under the penal code. Euthanasia is specifically not allowed, but assisting suicide is allowed if it is done for unselfish motives. No doctors are required, nor is any medical precondition. The only requirement is that the person who wishes to die be competent to make such a decision. Assisted suicides must be reported to the local authorities.

There are five right-to-die organizations in Switzerland:

- EXIT Deutsche Schweiz
- EXIT Association pour le Droit de Mourir dans la Dignité
- DIGNITAS
- EXIT International
- lifecircle

The last three of these will offer assisted suicide to non-residents.

The protocol set up by these organizations does require

examination by a doctor, who will assess the patient's mental condition and decisional capacity. The doctor may then prescribe a lethal dose of drugs, which will be held by the organization until the day of use, at which time a volunteer will again assess decisional capacity, and if the patient is competent and still wants to die, the drugs will mixed in liquid or food for the patient to swallow.

Assisted deaths in Switzerland account for 0.45% of deaths there, as opposed to 0.39% in the Netherlands and 0.09% in Oregon.

9) Luxembourg
Euthanasia is illegal but physician-assisted suicide is permitted through an act similar to the Belgian act.

10) Colombia
In 1997 Colombia's Constitutional Court ruled that assisted death is permitted so long as it is performed by a medical professional with the consent of a terminally ill patient who is undergoing intense suffering. If these conditions are not met a penalty may be imposed for mercy killing, but the penalty is much less than for other homicides. The Court recommended that legislation should be passed regulating assisted suicide, but this is yet to happen.

COUNTERING THE CRITICS
In reading what critics have to say about the practices in other countries one must be aware of the fact that such criticisms would exist, whatever the truth about them. For the anti-euthanasia lobby, which bases many of its arguments against any form of assisted death on dire warnings of consequences, the data from other countries entirely undercuts

the thrust of their jeremiadian warnings. So there is intense effort put into discrediting the evidence from these other jurisdictions — that the systems set up work very well, with minimal abuse.

Some of the attempts to discredit the assisted death practices in other countries are simply ill-informed. American Rick Santorum, a former senator from Pennsylvania and a leading Republican candidate for president in 2102, made the following statement at the American Heartland Forum in Columbus, Missouri, February 3, 2012:

> *In the Netherlands, people wear different bracelets if they are elderly. And the bracelet is: 'Do not euthanize me' . . . they have voluntary euthanasia in the Netherlands, but half of the people who are euthanized — ten percent of all deaths in the Netherlands — half of those people are euthanized involuntarily at hospitals because they are older and sick. And so elderly people in the Netherlands don't go to the hospital. They go to another country, because they are afraid, because of budget purposes, they will not come out of that hospital if they go in there with sickness.*

None of these claims are true. The Dutch government objected, but probably had little effect on Santorum and his followers.

Santorum, of course, presents an extreme example of the critics, and there are more sophisticated critics who claim to have scientifically based evidence that safeguards do not work. However, Justice Smith deals with these critics in a thorough and systematic analysis, summarized in the following points.

IMPACT OF LEGALIZATION OF ASSISTED DEATH ON THE VULNERABLE

This idea of course was central to the defeat of Sue Rodriguez's plea for mercy from the Supreme Court of Canada. It was well acknowledged that her disability prevented her from having the same right as able-bodied people in regard to committing suicide, but it was thought that changing the law would create too great a risk to vulnerable populations. Anything other than a blanket prohibition of assisted suicide was thought to be too risky.

Smith looked carefully at a study called "Legal physician-assisted suicide in Oregon and the Netherlands: evidence concerning the impact on 'vulnerable' groups." The authors of the study took the matter of vulnerable groups very seriously, partly because the concern comes up so often and partly because, if true, it should be recognized. They looked at groups usually defined as vulnerable: the elderly; women; uninsured persons; persons with AIDS; persons with low educational status; the poor; racial and ethnic minorities; persons with physical or mental disabilities or chronic non-terminal illnesses; minors and mature minors; and persons with psychiatric illnesses, including depression.

The authors, after examining much evidence, concluded that, with one exception, the rates of assisted suicide in both Oregon and the Netherlands show no evidence of increased risk to any of the identified groups, as compared with background populations. The one exception was people with AIDS, who showed a higher than normal rate of dying. However, the data predates the development of antiretroviral therapies that make AIDS much less of a death sentence.

The authors conclude with:

Thus, we found no evidence to justify the grave and important concern often expressed about the potential for abuse — namely, the fear that legalised physician-assisted dying will target the vulnerable or pose the greatest risk to people in vulnerable groups . . . it does show that there is no current factual support for so-called slippery-slope concerns about the risks of legalisation of assisted dying — concerns that death in this way would be practised more frequently on persons in vulnerable groups.

Smith gives much space to examining inevitable criticisms of the practices in other jurisdictions and then concludes with:

. . . the expert opinion evidence from persons who have done research into the question is that . . . the predicted abuse and disproportionate impact on vulnerable populations has not materialized . . . although none of the systems has achieved perfection, empirical researchers and practitioners who have experience in those systems are of the view that they work well in protecting patients from abuse while allowing competent patients to choose the timing of their deaths.

IMPACT ON PALLIATIVE CARE

One of the often-cited concerns by critics of legalization of assisted death is that less attention will then be given to palliative care. Again, evidence from other jurisdictions did not support that concern. One researcher said:

> *It is also worthwhile to comment on the relation between society's commitment to (palliative) care and euthanasia. It is sometimes argued that euthanasia cannot be made available to people in vulnerable groups because that would lessen pressures for improvement of their background circumstances. What is particularly disturbing about this argument is the usually tacit assumption that the suffering of those who are in vulnerable circumstances where euthanasia cannot be allowed, will serve as leverage for improving the provision of such things as adequate terminal care, adequate pain control, and the like. The evidence appears to be the other way around. Pain management was improving in the Netherlands before euthanasia was fully legalized, but has continued to do so at an increasingly rapid rate since legalization. It is legalization, or the prospect of immediate legalization, which appears to contribute to the improvement of terminal care and pain control.*

IMPACT ON PHYSICIAN-PATIENT RELATIONSHIP

Another general concern for critics of assisted death has been that legalizing physician-assisted death might negatively impact the physician-patient relationship. Arguments go along these lines: misconceptions might be spread, such as thinking that the main purpose of opioids would be to shorten life, and that administering a drug with the intent to end life is inconsistent with the goals and core activities of medicine.

Evidence, however, did not support these concerns. One doctor reported:

> *The blanket prohibition against physician-assisted dying discourages patients who are contemplating a hastened death from talking to their physicians, further isolating these patients. After all, if patients cannot speak openly and honestly to their doctors about end of life issues, then who will they speak to? The burden of secrecy is yet another burden that the already suffering patient is forced to bear.*

After evaluating the evidence Smith wrote:

> *My review of the evidence leads me to conclude with respect to impact on the doctor-patient relationship, that patients' trust in their physicians, and physicians' commitment to their patients' well-being, would not necessarily change for the worse if the law permitted physician-assisted death in highly constrained circumstances. The risk of misconceptions and distrust may be counterbalanced by the possibility of enhanced trust arising from more open communications. In brief, it is likely that the relationship would change, but the net effect could prove to be neutral or for the good.*

* * *

Smith concludes her section on other jurisdictions by writing:

> *My review of the evidence in this section, and in the preceding section on the experience in permissive jurisdictions, leads me to conclude that the risks inherent in permitting physician-assisted death can be identified and very substantially minimized through a carefully-designed system imposing stringent limits that are scrupulously monitored and enforced.*

The evidence collected by Justice Smith shows that the fears that are widely expressed about setting up a safe and workable system here in Canada are unfounded. Joe Arvay has outlined a plan that would work for Canada (see end of Chapter 6).

The experience of other countries should do much to counter the fears that have surrounded this issue for years in Canada, and which were directly responsible for the decision to deprive Sue Rodriguez of the legal right to have assistance in her death, and which prevented many thousands of ailing Canadians from having access to assistance in a gentle death.

SOURCES

Complete details and documentation of the B.C. Supreme Court case, with full details about other countries, are at the website for the B.C. Civil Liberties Association: bccla.org/our-work/blog/death-with-dignity-case.

Other sources:

www.cbc.ca/news/canada/assisted-suicide-where-do-canada-and-other-countries-stand-1.2795041.

"Final Certainty," *The Economist*, June 27, 2015.

APPENDIX 5
THE RULING OF THE SUPREME COURT OF CANADA — FEBRUARY 6, 2015

Held: The appeal should be allowed. Section 241 (b) and s. 14 of the *Criminal Code* unjustifiably infringe s. 7 of the *Charter* and are of no force or effect to the extent that they prohibit physician-assisted death for a competent adult person who (1) clearly consents to the termination of life and (2) has a grievous and irremediable medical condition (including an illness, disease or disability) that causes enduring suffering that is intolerable to the individual in the circumstances of his or her condition. The declaration of invalidity is suspended for 12 months. Special costs on a full indemnity basis are awarded against Canada throughout. The Attorney General of British Columbia will bear responsibility for 10 percent of the costs at trial on a full indemnity basis and will pay the costs associated with its presence at the appellate levels on a party-and-party basis.

The trial judge was entitled to revisit this Court's decision in *Rodriguez*. Trial courts may reconsider settled rulings of higher courts in two situations: (1) where a new legal issue is raised; and (2) where there is a change in the circumstances or evidence that fundamentally shifts the parameters of the debate. Here, both conditions were met. The argument before the trial judge involved a different legal conception of s. 7 than that prevailing when *Rodriguez* was decided. In particular, the law relating to the principles of overbreadth and gross disproportionality had materially advanced since *Rodriguez*. The matrix of legislative and social facts in this case also differed from the evidence before the Court in *Rodriguez*.

The prohibition on assisted suicide is, in general, a valid exercise of the federal criminal law power under s. 91(27) of the *Constitution Act, 1867*, and it does not impair the protected core of the provincial jurisdiction over health. Health is an area of concurrent jurisdiction, which suggests that aspects of physician-assisted dying may be the subject of valid legislation by both levels of government, depending on the circumstances and the focus of the legislation. On the basis of the record, the interjurisdictional immunity claim cannot succeed.

Insofar as they prohibit physician-assisted dying for competent adults who seek such assistance as a result of a grievous and irremediable medical condition that causes enduring and intolerable suffering, ss. 241 (b) and 14 of the *Criminal Code* deprive these adults of their right to life, liberty and security of the person under s. 7 of the *Charter*. The right to life is engaged where the law or state action imposes death or an increased risk of death on a person, either directly or indirectly. Here, the prohibition deprives some individuals of life, as it has the effect of forcing some individuals to take their own lives prematurely, for fear that they would be incapable of doing so when they reached the point where suffering was intolerable. The rights to liberty and security of the person, which deal with concerns about autonomy and quality of life, are also engaged. An individual's response to a grievous and irremediable medical condition is a matter critical to their dignity and autonomy. The prohibition denies people in this situation the right to make decisions concerning their bodily integrity and medical care and thus trenches on their liberty. And by leaving them to endure intolerable suffering, it impinges on their security of the person.

The prohibition on physician-assisted dying infringes the right to life, liberty and security of the person in a manner that is not in accordance with the principles of fundamental justice. The object of the prohibition is not, broadly, to preserve life whatever the circumstances, but more specifically to protect vulnerable persons from being induced to commit suicide at a time of weakness. Since a total ban on assisted suicide clearly helps achieve this object, individuals' rights are not deprived arbitrarily. However, the prohibition catches people outside the class of protected persons. It follows that the limitation on their rights is in at least some cases not connected to the objective and that the prohibition is thus overbroad. It is unnecessary to decide whether the prohibition also violates the principle against gross disproportionality.

Having concluded that the prohibition on physician-assisted dying violates s. 7, it is unnecessary to consider whether it deprives adults who are physically disabled of their right to equal treatment under s. 15 of the *Charter*.

Sections 241(b) and 14 of the *Criminal Code* are not saved

by s. 1 of the *Charter*. While the limit is prescribed by law
and the law has a pressing and substantial objective, the
prohibition is not proportionate to the objective. An absolute prohibition on physician-assisted dying is rationally
connected to the goal of protecting the vulnerable from
taking their life in times of weakness, because prohibiting
an activity that poses certain risks is a rational method of
curtailing the risks. However, as the trial judge found, the
evidence does not support the contention that a blanket
prohibition is necessary in order to substantially meet the
government's objective. The trial judge made no palpable
and overriding error in concluding, on the basis of evidence
from scientists, medical practitioners, and others who are
familiar with end-of-life decision-making in Canada and
abroad, that a permissive regime with properly designed and
administered safeguards was capable of protecting vulnerable people from abuse and error. It was also open to her to
conclude that vulnerability can be assessed on an individual
basis, using the procedures that physicians apply in their
assessment of informed consent and decisional capacity in
the context of medical decision-making more generally.
The absolute prohibition is therefore not minimally impair-
ing. Given this conclusion, it is not necessary to weigh the
impacts of the law on protected rights against the beneficial
effect of the law in terms of the greater public good.

The appropriate remedy is not to grant a free-standing
constitutional exemption, but rather to issue a declaration
of invalidity and to suspend it for 12 months. Nothing in
this declaration would compel physicians to provide assistance in dying. The *Charter* rights of patients and physicians
will need to be reconciled in any legislative and regulatory
response to this judgment.

The appellants are entitled to an award of special costs on a full indemnity basis to cover the entire expense of bringing this case before the courts. A court may depart from the usual rule on costs and award special costs where two criteria are met. First, the case must involve matters of public interest that are truly exceptional. It is not enough that the issues raised have not been previously resolved or that they transcend individual interests of the successful litigant: they must also have a significant and widespread societal impact. Second, in addition to showing that they have no personal, proprietary or pecuniary interest in the litigation that would justify the proceedings on economic grounds, the plaintiffs must show that it would not have been possible to effectively pursue the litigation in question with private funding. Finally, only those costs that are shown to be reasonable and prudent will be covered by the award of special costs. Here, the trial judge did not err in awarding special costs in the truly exceptional circumstances of this case. It was also open to her to award 10 percent of the costs against the Attorney General of British Columbia in light of the full and active role it played in the proceedings. The trial judge was in the best position to determine the role taken by that Attorney General and the extent to which it shared carriage of the case.

SELECT BIBLIOGRAPHY

Other references for specific points can be found in Chapter Notes and in Appendices Sources.

Bauslaugh, Gary. *Robert Latimer: A Story of Justice and Mercy* (Toronto: Lorimer, 2010).

Bauslaugh, Gary. *The Secret Power of Juries* (Toronto: Lorimer, 2013).

Bauslaugh, Gary. "The Trial of Evelyn Martens." *Humanist Perspectives* no. 152 (Spring 2005).

Bauslaugh, Gary. "When Trusted Information Sources go Wrong." *Humanist Perspectives* no. 161 (Summer 2007).

Bayda, Chief Justice of Saskatchewan. "Appeal Court Decision in R. v. Latimer." 1995 CanLII 3993 SKC.A.

Bennett, Gillian. "Dead at Noon." www.deadatnoon.com.

Carter v. Canada. Supreme Court of Canada hearing, transcript available through: www.scc-csc.gc.ca/case-dossier/info/search-recherche-eng.aspx.

Carter v. Canada. Supreme Court of Canada ruling: scc-csc. lexum.com/scc-csc/scc-csc/en/item/14637/index.do.

The Catholic Encyclopedia. www.newadvent.org/cathen/074 41a.htm.

Dixon, John. "Affidavit for B.C. Supreme Court in *Carter v. Canada.*" bccla.org/wp-content/uploads/2012/06/20110830-Affidavit-Carter-BCCLA-Affidavit.pdf.

Downie, Jocelyn. *Dying Justice* (Toronto: University of

Toronto Press, 2004).

Heinrich, Jeff. "Bill 52: A Timeline." www.montrealgazette .com/health/Bill+timeline/9510618/story.html.

Hofsess, John. *Last Rights*. Issues 1-17 published in the 1990s by The Right to Die Society of Canada. Edited by John Hofsess. Copies are difficult to find.

Hofsess, John. "Candle in the Wind." *Homemaker's Magazine* (Nov./Dec. 1991).

Hofsess, John. "Educating the world about choice-in-dying." *Last Rights*, Issue 14 (1995).

Hofsess, John. "Who Cares?" *Last Rights*, Issue 6, Oct./Nov. 1992.

Humphry, Derek. *Final Exit* (New York: Dell, 1992; 3rd. ed., 2002).

Kluge, Eike-Henner. *Ethics in Health Care: A Canadian Focus* (Toronto: Pearson, 2013).

Leenen case: www.canlii.org/en/on/onsc/doc/2000/2000can lii22380/2000canlii22380.html.

Libick, Helen. "Remembering Sue." *Last Rights*, Issue 13, Fall 1994.

Low, Donald. Video released after his death: www.cbc.ca/ news/canada/toronto/sars-doctor-donald-low-s-posthumous-plea-for-assisted-suicide-1.1866332.

McLuhan, Sabrina. "Sue Rodriguez fires Hofsess." *The Interim*. www.theinterim.com/issues/euthanasia-suicide/ sue-rodriguez-fires-hofsess.

Ogden, Russel. "Death Hastening and Canada's Inuit." *Last Rights*, Issue 15 (undated but probably 1996).

Ontario Justice Education Network. "Section 1 of the Charter and the Oakes Test." ojen.ca/resource/980.

Parliament of Canada. "Health and the *Constitution Act, 1867*." www.parl.gc.ca/content/lop/researchpublications/

prb0858-e.htm.

Rauh Jr., Joseph, and James Turner. "MIKULTRA Experiments in Montreal." coat.ncf.ca/our_magazine/links/issue43/articles/1957_1961_canada.htm.

Rodriguez Hearing, Supreme Court of Canada, available through: scc-csc.gc.ca.

Rodriguez ruling, Supreme Court of Canada. "*Rodriguez v. British Columbia* (1993) 3 SCR 519."

Smith, Lynn. "Reasons for Judgment, *Carter v. Canada.*" www.canlii.org/en/bc/bcsc/doc/2012/2012bcsc886/2012bcsc886.html.

Smith, Margaret. "The Rodriguez Case." Law and Government Division (October 1993) publications. gc.ca/Collection-R/LoPBdP/BP/bp349-e.htm.

Society, the Individual, and Medicine. "Suicide in Canada." www.med.uottawa.ca/sim/data/Suicide_e.htm.

Special Prosecutor's Report on Rodriguez Death. News release, B.C. Ministry of the Attorney General, June 28, 1995. Available at Law Library, University of Victoria.

Special Senate Committee on Euthanasia and Assisted Suicide. "Of Life and Death." www.parl.gc.ca/content/sen/committee/351/euth/rep/lad-a2-e.htm#l.

Sumner, Wayne. "The Morgentaler Effect." *The Walrus* (January/February 2011).

Truelove, Graham. *Svend Robinson: A Life in Politics.* (Ottawa, New Star Books, 2013).

Willowbrook State School. "A Voice Beyond the Wall." willowbrookstateschool.blogspot.ca/p/history.html.

ACKNOWLEDGEMENTS

Special thanks, as always, to Gwyneth Evans for her diligent and insightful work on this manuscript. Much help in reviewing the manuscript was also given by Shirley Johnson, John Dixon and Gordon MacDonald. I am indebted to Jonathan Bennett, Diana Davidson, Eike-Henner Kluge, John Hofsess, Robert Latimer, Evelyn Martens, Russel Ogden and Ruth Von Fuchs for extended discussions and identification of useful sources.

Thanks to James Lorimer for his faith in my work and his patience in supporting this project, as well as for his excellent editorial assistance.

INDEX